Nathaniel Tarn

American Poetry Contemporary Bibliography Series
General Editor: Lee Bartlett

1. *Diane Wakoski,* by Robert Newton (1987)
2. *Nathaniel Tarn,* by Lee Bartlett (1987)
3. *Jerome Rothenberg,* by Harry Polkinhorn (1988)
4. *Clayton Eshleman,* by Martha J. Sattler (1988)

Nathaniel Tarn
A Descriptive Bibliography

by
Lee Bartlett

American Poetry Contemporary Bibliography Series, No. 2

McFarland & Company, Inc., Publishers
Jefferson, North Carolina, and London

Frontispiece drawing of Nathaniel Tarn by Henri Seigle.

Foreword by Nathaniel Tarn first published in *American Poetry* 1, 2 (Winter 1984). Reproduced by permission.

Photographs and comments of Nathaniel Tarn reproduced by permission of Nathaniel Tarn.

Library of Congress Cataloguing-in-Publication Data

Bartlett, Lee, 1950–
  Nathaniel Tarn : a descriptive bibliography.

  (American poetry contemporary bibliography series ; no. 2)
  Includes index.
  1. Tarn, Nathaniel — Bibliography.   I. Title.
II. Series.
Z8858.97.B37   1987   016.821'914   87-43064
[PR6070.A57]

ISBN 0-89950-296-2 (acid-free natural paper) ∞

Printed in the United States of America.

McFarland   Box 611   Jefferson NC 28640

Contents

Preface   ix
Chronology   1
Foreword by Nathaniel Tarn   5

A. Books, Pamphlets, Broadsides   23
B. Items Edited, Translated, Introduced   57
C. Contributions to Periodicals   72
D. Translations by Nathaniel Tarn   88
E. Contributions to Anthologies   90
Appendix 1: Heteronyms   95
Appendix 2: Cape Editions   103
Appendix 3: Criticism and Reviews   106

Title Index   119

Preface

Nathaniel Tarn, called by Kenneth Rexroth "one of the most outstanding poets of his generation . . . a part of international literature," is a prolific poet, translator, editor, and essayist. Books of poetry like *The Beautiful Contradictions, Lyrics for the Bride of God,* and *The House of Leaves* rank as powerful and influential contemporary collections, while Tarn's translations of the work of Pablo Neruda remain standard. He created and served as general editor for the Cape Editions series, one of the most daring and successful publishing ventures since the war, and currently holds editorial and consulting positions on *Conjunctions* (New York), *Po&Sie* (Paris), and *Modern Poetry in Translation* (London). Further, a specialist in the Highland Maya and in the sociology of Buddhist institutions, as E. Michael Mendelson he has published extensively in those areas.

The present volume attempts to record all books, pamphlets, and broadsides written, edited, introduced, and translated by Nathaniel Tarn through 1986. In addition, the poet's periodical appearances are noted, as are his contributions to anthologies and work published under the "heteronyms" Michel Tavriger and E. Michael Mendelson. The compilation ends with an annotated checklist of criticism and a checklist of selected reviews.

Section A describes all first editions of the poet's books, pamphlets, and broadsides published as Nathaniel Tarn. A typical entry contains the following information:

Edition statement: The initial heading of each entry identifies title, date of publication, and edition.

Title page: A quasi-facsimile transcription of the title page.

Collation: Pagination shows the numbering or inferred numbering of each page; size of item in inches; type of paper, whether laid or wove. As almost all of Tarn's books have been produced by modern machine methods, I have not collated signatures.

Pagination: Contents of each page, often described in quasi-facsimile.

Binding: Color of cloth; quasi-facsimile transcription of all printing or stamping on covers and spine; description of endpapers.

Dust jacket: Color of paper and printing; quasi-facsimile transcription of printing on covers and spine, as well as flyleaves.

Publication: Available facts concering publication, including publisher, date published, and price.

Contents: List of poems and/or articles included.

Notes: In March 1987, the compiler interviewed Nathaniel Tarn at his home in Santa Fe, New Mexico. The poet commented on the publishing history of several of his books, with the warning that he was working without notes and his memory might not be quite accurate. Those comments follow a number of entries.

Section B includes books edited, translated, and introduced by Tarn; it is descriptive as above. Section C includes the poet's contributions to periodicals; at the head of each entry distinction is made between poetry and prose. Section D draws together material Tarn has translated for either periodical or anthology publication, while Section E lists the poet's contributions to anthologies. Appendix 1 lists books and periodical publications under the poet's two "heteronyms"; ideally, such material would appear in the bibliography proper, but the poet requested that in this case it be relegated to an appendix. Appendix 2 gives background to the Cape Editions series, providing a list of volumes published under Tarn's editorship. Appendix 3 offers an annotated checklist of criticism, as well as a checklist of reviews.

I would like to thank Nathaniel Tarn for giving me free run of his collection of first editions, magazines, and manuscripts during the preparation of this volume, as well as for permission to reprint several photographs. And again, of course, my wife Mary.

Chronology

1928 Born Paris, France, June 30.

1935 Family moves to Belgium. Attends French-speaking Lycée d' Anvers.

1939 Moves to England. Living at Colwyn Bay, Wales, when war is declared. London during height of Blitz. Attends Clifton Preparatory School, Bristol, Gloucestershire; Buxton Secondary School and Holm Leigh Preparatory School at Buxton, Derbyshire; later Clifton College, at Bude and Bristol.

1946 Scholar in History at King's College, Cambridge; studies History with Butterfield and Postan, English with Leavis. Visits to Paris, Spain, and Italy. Graduates with B.A. (Honors).

1948 Moves to Paris. Continues studies on Dante and medieval philosophy. Works part-time on Tourist Guide "This Week in Paris." Enrolls in anthropological courses at the Musée de l'Homme with partial "License" in anthropology, subsequently in the Centre de Formation aux Recherches Ethnologiques, with Certificate of the C.F.R.E. and in the Vth section of the Ecole des Hautes Etudes (Elève Titulaire). Studies with Marcel Griaule, Germaine Dieterlen, Pierre Métais, André Leroi-Gourhan, Paul Lévy, and Claude Lévi-Strauss. Catalogues Assam Naga collection at the Museum; thesis on Tiger myths of the Assam Naga. First published article on Supervielle commissioned by Georges Bataille at *Critique*. Attends André Breton's Surrealist group with Henri and No Seigle and Octavio Paz.

1950 *La Légende de Saint-Germain-des-Prés.*

1951 Smith-Mundt-Fulbright scholar in anthropology to the University of Chicago. Fulbright "orientation" at Yale with Diploma in American Studies. Visits with Ralph Linton, George Murdoch, Abraham Kardiner, Matthew Stirling, Alfred Kroeber, Julian Steward, and other anthropologists. At Chicago, studies for doctorate with Robert Redfield, Milton Singer, Fred Eggan, Sol Tax.

1952 Research assistant to Robert Redfield. M.A. Degree in anthropology. Vacations in Cuba; arrives on day of Batista's last coup d'état. Studies *santería* with Wilfredo Lam. Sent by Robert Redfield to Atitlán, Guatemala, and picks Santiago Atitlán for fieldwork. Travels extensively in Guatemala, Mexico, collecting textiles. Visits with Miguel Covarrubias, Steve de Borhegyi, Alfonso Caso, Diego Rivera, Maurice Herzog, and others.

1953   Return to London. Postgraduate student and, later, part-time Lecturer at London School of Economics. Studies with Raymond Firth, Isaac Schapera, S.F. Nadel, Maurice Freedman.

1957   Ph.D. University of Chicago, with thesis on "Religion and World-View in Santiago Atitlán"; publication prevented by death of Robert Redfield. Studies Burmese and Pali.

1958   Rockefeller Foundation Grant, mediated by Royal Institute of International Affairs, London, to Burma. Works on religion and politics, and esoteric ("messianic") Buddhism, mainly in Rangoon and Mandalay. Travels: Kachin Hills, Shan States, Chindwin area, Pagan and Central Burma, Karen areas, Mergui-Tenasserim. Frequent visits with Gordon Luce and J.S. Furnivall. U.K. delegate to World Fellowship of Buddhists, Bangkok. Returns to London via Cambodia, India, Nepal, Iran, Turkey, and Greece in winter of 1959.

1960   Lecturer in Southeast Asian Anthropology, School of Oriental and African Studies, University of London, until 1966. Attends many professional conferences.

1961   Convenes seminar on Problems in the Sociology of Theravada Buddhist institutions at the 10th Pacific Science Congress, Hawaii. Passes through San Francisco and buys up much little press material at City Lights. After Hawaii, survey work on "new religions" in Kyoto, Okayama Province, and Tokyo. Introduced by David Wevill to "The Group," run by Edward Lucie-Smith, with George MacBeth, Peter Porter, Philip Hobsbaum, Peter Redgrove, Fleur Adcock, and others. Meets Ted Hughes, Christopher Middleton, John Digby, Alberto de Lacerda, etc.

1963   Wins First Guinness Prize for Poetry at Cheltenham Festival. Recommended from there by John Fowles to Tom Maschler at Jonathan Cape, Ltd. Berlin Conference on Poetry and Communication. Meets Stephen Spender, W.H. Auden, Langston Hughes, Vasco Popa, and Gunter Grass. Begins to advise Cape on poetry.

1964   *Old Savage/Young City.*

1965   *Thirteen to Bled, Penguin Modern Poets 7, Los Escándalos de Maximón.*

1966   *The Heights of Macchu Picchu.*

1967   Resigns from London University and joins Jonathan Cape, Ltd.,
        as General Editor of Cape Editions, Founding Director of
        Cape-Goliard Press, and general advisor to the list. Friendships
        with George Steiner, Hugh MacDiarmid, Tony Richardson,
        Arnold Wesker, Mary Hutchinson, and others. Frequent travel
        to America; visits Louis Zukofsky, Robert Duncan, Charles
        Olson, John Berryman, Pablo Neruda, Edward Dorn, Allen
        Ginsberg, Nicanor Parra, Jonathan Williams, Toby Olson,
        Kenneth Rexroth, William Everson, and Kenneth Patchen.
        Travels Canadian Pacific from Calgary to Vancouver and gives
        first reading on continent at Simon Frazer under auspices of
        Robin Blaser. *Where Babylon Ends.*

1968   *Selected Poems of Kenneth Patchen.*

1969   Services dispensed with by Jonathan Cape, Ltd. Visiting Pro-
        fessor of English, S.U.N.Y. Buffalo, with Anselm Hollo, James
        Wright, and John Knoepfle. Surfaces at Panajachel, Guate-
        mala, where he spends six months writing *A Nowhere for Vallejo.*
        The Beautiful Contradictions, October, Con Cuba, Victor Segalen:
        Stelae.

1970   Immigrates into U.S. as Visiting Fellow, Council of Humanities
        and Visiting Lecturer with rank of Professor, Department of
        Romance Languages, Princeton University. Frequent read-
        ings; meets Gary Snyder at Notre Dame Literary Festival.
        Visiting Professor, Department of Comparative Literature,
        Rutgers. *October: The Silence, Pablo Neruda: Selected Poems.*

1971   Visiting Professor, Writers' Conference, University of Colorado.
        A Nowhere for Vallejo.

1972   Tenured Professorship, Rutgers.

1973   *Lyrics for the Bride of God: Section: The Artemision.*

1974   Festival of the Arts, University of Oregon; Northwestern Festival.
        The Persephones.

1975   First visit to Alaska (continued visits in 1976 and 1977 on Lindblad
        Explorer, as Lecturer, to the Aleutians and Hokkaido). First
        International Cambridge University Poetry Festival. *Lyrics for
        the Bride of God, Sangha and State in Burma: A Study of Monastic Sec-
        tarianism and Leadership.*

1976   Visiting Lecturer, Department of Folklore, University of Pennsyl-
        vania. *The House of Leaves.*

1977   *The Microcosm, The Ground of Our Great Admiration.*

1978   Archeology at Cuello (Belize), Mesa Redonda de Palenque. *Bird-
        scapes, with Seaside, The Forest.*

1979   Spends year in Santiago Atitlán, Guatemala, with grants from
        Wenner Gren Foundation and Social Science Research Coun-
        cil of New York. *Atitlan/Alashka.*

1980   Poets in the Schools Program, Pennsylvania.

1981   *The Landsongs.*

1982   Graduate Faculty of Anthropology, Rutgers, with teaching in Archeology Program, Douglass College. Visiting Professor in American Literature and Ethnohistory, Jilin University, People's Republic of China. Extensive travel in China and Mongolia. Acting Chairman, Department of Comparative Literature, Rutgers. *Weekends in Mexico.*

1983   Sabbatical in Pojoaque and El Rancho, County of Santa Fe, New Mexico.

1984   Tara Tulku Rimpoche seminars in New York and Amherst, with Robert Thurman. Philosophy of Keiji Nishitani conference at Amherst and Smith. Takes early retirement from Rutgers. *The Desert Mothers.*

1985   Moves to Las Dos, Santa Fe, New Mexico. Ezra Pound Conference, California State University at San Jose. *At the Western Gates.*

1986   Frequent readings in Europe, New Mexico, and California.

Foreword: "Child as Father to Man in the American Uni-verse"

by Nathaniel Tarn

Last year I received a letter from a member of the English department at a university in Philadelphia. She informed me that she had been asked to write an article on my work for a prominent dictionary of literary biography. She had been working all summer and had been most impressed. Could we meet for detailed discussions? I called for a pleasant talk. After a while, she revealed that I was to be included in the volume on postwar British poets. I said that I had now been here twelve years, was a citizen, and had been a champion of American poetry, even in England, for ten years before that. She was very sorry. She had even been preparing a conference paper as well. Her editor called later: would I not reconsider this "foolish casting away of a chance at an academic reputation?" I talked about the virtues of consistency. He put down the phone with a marked, sorrowful finality. A terminal case. I have never heard another word about the matter.

There had been other occasions on which I'd found myself to be a "job" to do. Yet, over the years, I had begun to wonder whether, once past the Statue of Liberty, the tired, poor, huddled and yearning poet stood a chance in hell of ever really being accepted in America. A curious business. You read that a kind judge will finally give an illiterate old Russian his citizenship without a word of English to his credit. But the poet? *No Señor!* Citizenship maybe; status of American Poet, *niet*. And this is the last country on earth you are supposed to be able to CHOOSE. Picking up from William Carlos Williams on the Americans and the British, that is what I want to talk about in this piece.

Quelques précisions: Britain was kind to me and, indirectly, saved my life. At best, however, my Britannicity has always been marginal. I was born in Paris of a French-Rumanian mother and a British-Lithuanian father. I was there seven years and then a further four in a French-speaking *Lycée* in Belgium. I arrived in England a week before WWII. I was an alien and started into my first English classrooms with something like terror. I was

5

Nathaniel Tarn, 1944.

called "Frog." Of course, I was marked by public school (British: private) and later by Cambridge.

During the Blitz in England (Cumberland Hotel, London, right next to the AA batteries in Hyde Park), the only book I had managed to read was a child's life of Abraham Lincoln. The Blitz took away my Latin and my violin but it left me Lincoln. Just before the Blitz: why had everyone in my dorm been whispered at one evening or another and disappeared the next morning . . . to America? Except myself. After the Blitz: Cornwall and a school-life like a military camp's. The Surrealists I devoured with a passion I imagined to be all dead in a time as old as Mycenae. They did not save me from constant depression. What did was the history of the Pilgrims in, of all things, Nevins and Commager. There was a U.S. flag at a base some twenty minutes from the school: I would go to watch it as often as I could in the evening when it was ceremonially lowered. On my dorm wall, I had a *Daily Telegraph* map of the United States and I learned the capitals of the forty-eight by heart. An understanding biology teacher lent me some American literature: James Thurber is all I can remember of that. On the English side, a passion for Virginia Woolf caused me to be accused of neglecting Shakespeare!

I always read French for happiness and, in 1948, returned to Paris "forever." I also began a long, painful and losing battle with bilingualism. I wrote in French for some three years, trying to forget English. I frequented André Breton and the Surrealists and met Octavio Paz there. I then became a student of anthropology, working with Marcel Griaule, Germaine Dieterlen, André Leroi-Gourhan, Paul Lévy, above all with Claude Lévi-Strauss. In French, I achieved little more than twenty-fifth rate Apollinaire. I walked Paris deep into the night, imagining that I would die if I were ever sundered from it. Anthropology, most of which is written in English, sundered me.

In Paris, after two years of anthropology, it seemed you had to go abroad. By this time, I had adopted the fashionable stance of suspicion vis-à-vis the U.S. held by the overwhelming majority of European students. And yet it was to Chicago — after an inane "orientation" to the mysteries of American democracy at Yale — that a Smith-Mundt/Fulbright scholarship in anthropology finally led me. I crashed George Murdoch at Yale, as well as Ralph Linton (full of tales about Ruth Benedict's witchcraft); I crashed Abraham Kardiner in New York and lunched with Julian Steward and Alfred Kroeber at Columbia; I was treated to a Chinese lunch at the Smithsonian by Matthew Stirling and William Fenton, with a visit on the side to the B.I.A. At Chicago, there were Robert Redfield, Fred Eggan, Sol Tax, and Sal Washburn. Over at Northwestern University, where we (Claude Tardits, my roommate and I) would go to see a "real American campus, with real girls and real ice-cream," we followed William Herskovitz and William Bascom. The latter suggested a working vacation in Havana: I arrived, coincidentally, on the day Batista took over for the last time, met Wilfredo Lam and Alfredo Ortiz and studied *Santeria.*

On the Chicago campus, there seemed to be no way of contacting anyone literary: finishing a Ph.D. requirement in one year flat kept us busy eighteen hours a day. We endured the grey Gothic, learned to say "I love you" to the U. of C. girls, and the peripatetic Paul Radin (possibly a kinsman of mine) virtually lived in our apartment. Somewhere, like a needle in several dozen haystacks, lay the information which could conceivably have led me to Black Mountain College. Instead, in June 1952, I went for a year's field work to Central America. There is a movie — *The Last Picture Show,* I believe — which has the sound track of precisely that year at Chicago. I wish I could see it, say, every three years.[1] By this time, I wrote in English again and France seemed to be out of the question. British anthropology was in its most virulent Social-Anthropology-Only phase and I was told by more than one practitioner that I had better bury all thoughts of poetry if I wanted a career in the field.

Larvatus Prodeo: I assumed a sea-change. For many years, nothing further was said. Life revolved around Raymond Firth, Isaac Schapera, S.F. Nadel, Edmund Leach, Maurice Freedman, Christoph von Führer-Haimendorf at the London School of Economics and the School of Oriental and African Studies. Tea with Arthur Waley provided a welcome change.

Six years later, back from an exhausting eighteen months of fieldwork in Burma, a young Canadian poet met there in Mandalay, David Wevill, took me to the Friday evening sessions of a group called The Group. It met in the house of Edward Lucie-Smith, who later left poetry for art criticism. Over tea and cookies, the likes of Philip Hobsbaum, Peter Redgrove, George MacBeth, and Peter Porter politely tore the guts out of each other's poems, the custom being for one poet per evening to have some six or seven poems mimeographed for discussion. Sensing little in all this beyond a neo-"Movement" social faction (with the likes of Philip Larkin putting me to sleep up there), I stayed on for a while, for the sake of literary companionship, missing as I did the amenities of the Parisian café. The Group was kind to me, however. Through MacBeth's contacts at the BBC, I was eventually chosen to be the Group poet presented on the Third Programme, with the poems appearing in *The Listener.*

Little by little, a British "career" occurred. The First Guinness Prize for Poetry at Cheltenham — the first and last prize I have ever received — led to my first book with Jonathan Cape and, a year later, with Random House. This in turn, when I had left anthropology in 1967, led to two very productive years with Cape as Founding Director of the Cape-Goliard Press (it had been my idea to marry the creativity of Barry Hall and Tom Raworth's Goliard Press with the distributive capacities of Cape) and General Editor of Cape Editions — still remembered here as distributed by Grossman in New York. The work during those two years was substantial: some forty titles in Cape Editions (starting off with Lévi-Strauss, two Barthes and Olson's *Ishmael*); some twenty-five titles in Cape Goliard, including the standard Olson, and many authors ranging from Lévi-Strauss to Zukofsky in the general list. I was fired in 1969 on the ostensible ground that the books were not earning money, and Cape retreated back to the gentility from which it has never since moved one inch.

I don't exactly remember when the American shift began. Eliot, Pound, Cummings and some others went back to my schooldays. So did a passion for Henry James. In 1961, as convener of a seminar on the sociology of Theravada Buddhist institutions at the 10th Pacific Science Conference, I went to Hawaii, and on to Japan, via San Francisco. At City Lights bookstore, I bought myself blind: many things (later valuable as first editions), things I hardly knew anything about, seized up by pure instinct. Was this when I picked up Olson, probably *The Distances,* rather than the *Maximus Poems?* Or *Maximus to Dogtown?* Or McClure's *Dark Brown?* In any event, by 1963 or so, Jonathan Williams was in Hampstead, urging us on into unknown fields, making us buy up Peter Russell's American stocks at his ailing bookstore. The American Embassy still believed in readings in those days and had an excellent library for poetry and poetry records. Patchen's readings to jazz were a great discovery.

By 1967, I was hot to compete with Stuart Montgomery's Fulcrum Press for every one we could attract: Olson, Duncan, Zukofsky were those I called "my three pillars," but there were also Ginsberg, Blackburn, Snyder, McClure, Levertov, Jonathan Williams — among others. Some, like Creeley and Oppen, already had British publishers. This was also the time of the great Festival Hall poetry scenes where Olson read with such poets as Neruda and Ungaretti, though also, given English proclivities (Alvarez's *The New Poetry* with Penguin), with Robert Lowell or John Berryman. These were the years of many meetings: Zukofsky and Ginsberg in their dealings with Cape; Olson in London and, his first contract in my pocket, in Bled, Yugoslavia, after the Spoleto Festival, circa 1966; Ed Dorn at Essex; McClure when producing *The Beard* at the Royal Court . . . on a trip twice across the U.S. and Canada and back to say goodbye to anthropology and hello to editing: Paul Blackburn, Jonathan Williams, Toby Olson, Ronald Johnson, Robert Vas Dias at Aspen, Robert Duncan, Kenneth Rexroth, and William Everson reading *together* on Tamalpais and Kenneth Patchen (whose English *Selected Poems* I had suggested doing for Cape) at midnight in Palo Alto immediately after Tamalpais.

Two years later, in 1969, I began moving here by teaching a summer course at S.U.N.Y. Buffalo with fellow teachers Anselm Hollo and James Wright. Early in 1970, I immigrated as a Research Fellow, Council of the Humanities and Visiting Professor in Romance Languages at Princeton. By 1971, I was at Rutgers and became Distinguished Professor of Comparative Literature there, commuting from the Delaware River at New Hope, PA to New Brunswick, NJ. In these early days, I met Jerome Rothenberg in New York and was present with Dennis Tedlock at the birth of *Alcheringa* in Santa Fe; a friendship was also initiated with George Quasha at S.U.N.Y. Stony Brook. Richard Grossinger and *Io* were encountered in Vermont. Dr. Generosity's as a reading place in New York. Later: Robert Kelly at Bard. Snyder at a Notre Dame literary festival and on a visit to Princeton where I interviewed him for *Alcheringa*. The list is too long, but a context was forming: George Economou, Armand Schwerner, Michael Anania, John Matthias, Jack Shoemaker were among other early friends. Between then and now, I have visited every state in the union, including three consecutive summers in Alaska and many seasons in New Mexico. The land itself is the greatest love.

* * *

In the course of my six year long English literary life, I determined that: 1) English poetry had been virtually dead since Hopkins at best, or since Blake at worst; 2) British, as opposed to English, poetry was Celtic if it was anything, with poets like Yeats, MacDiarmid, David Jones and Dylan Thomas as the only ones I cared for deeply (in very varied ways) or was

marginal to mainstream English as in the case of Basil Bunting; 3) an international wandering *mestizo,* additionally Jewish, could be neither English nor
Celt; 4) the English language (all spoken versions of which since my first arrival in 1939 had seemed to me to be arbitrary, almost theatrical) could therefore live for me only in a new country, a chosen country; 5) the new country
in which energy was being put into the language was the U.S. of A.; 6) this
new country was available by its very charter and definition and seemed, on
the surface, most welcoming.

I know that here I am being unjust to a number of fine poets who
learned from the Pound-Williams tradition and, under cruel neglect for the
most part, persisted over the years in creating an English version of that
tradition: Roy Fisher, Gael Turnbull and some of their associates would be
among them. Somehow, none excited me as much as their American coun-
terparts, except perhaps J.H. Prynne.

Just as, in most religions, there seems to be a main, orthodox and legal-
istic church and a shadow, heterodox, perhaps mystical church, so there
seemed to be an America in England and an England in America. England
in America seemed to me to be covered by the term "academic" (against
which the "New Poetry," as defined by the Don Allen anthology, constantly
battled): its strongholds located in the Ivy League schools, their reading circuits and antiquated magazines, and in East Coast papers like the *New York
Times* and the *New York Review of Books.* Of course, it was more complex than
that. America in England was composed of the sacred trio I called the
"suicide club" as the overwhelmingly model-poets of the "Movement" and its
immediate successors. You could add what was known of the Pound-
Williams tradition and of the Beats. Charles Tomlinson, in the record of an
Englishman who remained one, quotes my *bête noire* among the neo–Movement people, Ian Hamilton, on his Zukofsky sumposium in Hamilton's
magazine *the Review:* "The editorial motive of *the Review* in this project has
been a documentary one. We believe that the Movement ought at least to
be known about."[2] The crass superciliousness of this, matched in a hundred
treatments of Black Mountain, Objectivism, the San Francisco Renaissance,
and other such American endeavors in papers like the *TLS* or magazines like
the Review could not be overcome: it could only be flown. Even today, the
pyramidal structure of the English poetry establishment has not yet been
broken despite years of courageous opposition.

I write this away from home in Pennsylvania with few references available. But I believe that the years 1967–9 were the decisive ones for me.
Despite the Americawards title poem of the first book, *Old Savage/Young City,*
and its successor, *Where Babylon Ends,* they must probably be accounted,
stylistically and structurally, as English books. The people I remember feeling close to at this time were poets such as Christopher Middleton, David
Wevill, some of Peter Redgrove and Jon Silkin, as well as younger writers,
more American-influenced, like Tom Raworth and Lee Harwood, and poet-

artists like John Digby, my close friend. The break came with the third book *The Beautiful Contradictions* in 1969 and an article: "World Wide Open: The Work Laid Before Us in This Disunited Kingdom."[3]

Despite opposition to "Little Englandism," the early poems remained tight, highly crafted ("wordsmithed") and "closed." The subject matter reached beyond England but the manner did not. One liberating force may have been Neruda—but less than has been said and supposed. More to the point: suddenly, one day, MacDiarmid was to read in London. I realized that I did not know his work. His *Collected Poems* (published in the States, of course, with a small Scottish edition) had recently become available. Here was a man who seemed like a mountain so tall that the English sheep grazing on his sides could not even see the mountain. Here was a long line, sanctioning the long breath-line which had already been noticed by some as a characteristic of my work. Here, above all, was a man who seemed able to put almost anything into a poem and with a straightforwardness at that, which appeared much more available than the esoteric reaches of Pound and Eliot. In the context of Little Englandism, it seemed almost impossible to go back to these two at that moment. It *did* seem possible to go forward to MacDiarmid, and I believe it is mainly under his impulse that *The Beautiful Contradictions* was written. Another "father figure" was Olson. Not so much, initially, the Olson of Maximus as the earlier poet of *The Distances,* to me, at the time, linguistically the most invigorating book of the post–Poundian era. Strangely, it was not until very much later that I came to Williams and I suffered from that lateness. For lyricism, I believe I am indebted to Patchen and Dylan Thomas and, behind them, to a number of Europeans such as Rilke, Lorca, Apollinaire, Breton, Supervielle.

The burden of "World Wide Open," then, was an attack on Little Englandism (see also part 14 of *The Beautiful Contradictions*) from three main directions: the Pound-Williams tradition and its associated movements in the "New American Poetry," the Celtic Belt and Regional England, the world of Latin America and Europe. The guideline for me was stated in part 1 of *The Beautiful Contradictions*: "We have no alternative to taking the whole world as our mother" (continuing: "since no one can pretend to own anything of permanence / or to anchor his roots in any particular plot / or speak in anything but borrowed languages"). The rest of the story is, in a sense, the attempt to match such universalism with the belief that America is a family of nations rather than a single nation; that this family alone offers a newcomer roots, and that, since everyone in America "borrows languages," someone like myself could aspire to be an American poet. Hence, the long periplus through the American continents in the wake of Pound as well as Olson's opening words in *Call me Ishmael.* This was to lead to such books as *Lyrics for the Bride of God, The House of Leaves, Alashka* (written jointly with Janet Rodney), *Palenque,* and the work in progress, *Seeing America First.* A prose piece, first printed in Richard Grossinger's *Io:* "Towards any

Geography, towards any American whatsoever," states rather cryptically the myth of the continental spine and its role in focusing the major part of this phase of work.[4] Letters received at this time, from major writers here in the traditions I respect, confirmed for me my belief in *The Beautiful Contradictions* as a turning point.

It takes an Englishman forever to welcome you, though when he does, it is usually for life. An American welcomes you immediately but knows in his sinews that America is mobile and will soon move you on to someplace else. It is also true that, immigrating in 1970, you were coming, without realizing it, into a boom time. With hindsight, opposition to the Vietnam war seemed immensely favorable to poetry: the revival of public readings launched by the "New Poetry" of the fifties and early sixties now reached its peak; bookstores flourished in the centers and in many regions; there seemed to be no end to literary festivals, circuits, little magazines.

There *was* an end, abrupt, almost tangible: the end of the war. Since that time, I have never once wished to leave this land which I love with a passion as great as that of any compatriot. Yet I know extremes of solitude and abandonment, the like of which seemed unthinkable at the time of arrival. Spread out over the immensity of the continent, we have each gone back, I guess, to our own solitudes. The history of our time in poetry is no doubt in the letters. Looking at the Olson-Creeley correspondence and many other such, it was like this, no doubt, as the "New Poetry" came to birth.[5]

A statement made circa 1969 sums up much of my biosphere at the time. It may be worth repeating here:

> Poetry for me is the discovery of a sound which arises out of unimpeded listening. The sound, once recognized, can assume a number of voices; my life-history happens to have given me no convincing English of my own. I have always been fascinated by the interplay between restricted and elaborated codes, between common parlances and formal rhetorics. Form is usually allowed to grow out of content, though I am aware of moving towards more and more open form as I discover that there is less and less that *cannot* be discussed in poetry. In the early work, my anthropological experience prompted me to speak out of various personae associated with *Old Savage;* an old, wise Amerindian or Melanesian, aware of what our culture has done to his, forgiving, sad at his own destruction principally because it mirrors the destruction of the whole natural earth. Dropping anthropology as a profession has enabled me to speak as an anthropologist and add the dialectic of observer and observed to the previous one-dimensional picture. As a result, politics have become a major factor in recent work such as *The Beautiful Contradictions.* This complex material is offset by simple lyrical-erotic sequences such as occur in *October.* The aim is to work towards more and more satisfactory resolutions of the tension between simplicity and complexity.
>
> We may be living at a time when only the exasperation of contradictions is possible for the artist; synthesis is closed to him because of the intolerable weight of new information he must shoulder each day. In this situation, poetry is more than ever a discipline, the means whereby a poet not only discovers, but literally creates, himself out of the total flux. Silence is more than

poetry's complement: it is that which poetry must sink back into the moment it ceases to perform this function. It follows that poetry for poetry's sake — decoration *et al.* — is intolerable.

Translation is (i) a duty within the Republic of Letters; (ii) a way of allowing various voices to speak; (iii) a means of letting air into the stale bed of English letters. Editorial activity is an extension of translation, not only from languages but from disciplines. *Transformation* is a key concept, linking early allegiances to Surrealism with present interests in Structuralism.[6]

* * *

Freedom of choice is the issue. Choice of land, people, form, line, breath, and voice. Here, the personal story is left behind and I look at available poetics. Now, how to deal with the now?

When leaving the Old World for the New, the problem of who is being addressed in poetry becomes for me the main one of all. In one, crucial sense we choose to address an elite or specialists (other poets or professional students of poetry) or a general reading public. My personal preference would go to both, but it rarely falls out that way.

And it is not, for me, a matter of the United States alone. It is, it has to be, a matter of the whole continent from Alaska to Tierra del Fuego. Therefore, it is a matter of ourselves as members of a polity and of those we choose to regard as aliens, or as underprivileged *others,* both outside and inside our borders. This, in turn, is a paradigm of the way we look at and treat the *other* throughout the universe.

Ultimately, it is a matter of what we should mean by "nation" — the dream of Rimbaud's "nations in joy" — the real meaning of "nation": local, regional, metropolitan, continental. And the meaning of universe. UNI-VERSE.

A very few have begun on this: notably, and nobly, Gary Snyder (though I often disagree with him on many issues). But this is for the future. I return to a narrower theme: the distinction between poetry addressed to an elite and poetry addressed to the people at large, or that small section of it which has not been consumerized out of existence as a reading and listening public. I am going to use academic labels, though most readers should be aware that contemporary poets reject them. Using such labels — and large ones at that — let's postulate, in elite-addressed poetry especially, a field of endeavor known as "modernism" and another known as "postmodernism." Few agree on definitions, especially of the latter. While the labels appear to be historically conditioned and sequential, I'm not sure that they do not also, perhaps predominatingly, represent alternative procedures, often present simultaneously in our practice. Try a model (all terms to be preceded by "relatively"):

"Modernism"	*"Postmodernism"*
Structural (Space)	Phenomenological (Time)
Cyclic (closed)	Linear (open)
Mythic	Scientific
General	Particular
Gnostic	Agnostic
International	Regional/Local
Traditional over	Individual over
Individual	Traditional

Of course, this rarely works in detail — but it's a start. Now follow a line of thought that might provide a common field of discourse for elite-addressed as well as more popular poetries. Take a major characteristic of "modernist" poetry and follow it through. Whether we come from archaeology, linguistics, and modern physics, as our major critic does, or from the atomization of the culture of our time, start with collage.[7] Collage and montage: the attempt to arrive at a product of imagination by smelting many small acts of acute attention to the data world of all time and all space into one vortical image. The structuralist move to lay out time in space so that it is all spread out together before us contemporaneously. In the hands of a Pound, an Eliot, a Joyce, the effort is intensely responsible, the choices are pedagogically selected; the textual products are backed by spectacular personal commitments, often to disastrously regressive causes. The primary responsibility is to an elite consensus regarding twenty centuries or more of universal human culture.

William Carlos Williams: "You see in American verse, especially in the modern phase, a struggle to establish itself *formally* among the literatures of the world."[8] My suspicion is that "postmodernism" — if the label is kept at all and *I* am clear that it should *not* be — may one day be seen in the main as a regional variation of "modernism," evolved by these our States and other western centers of culture under American cultural hegemony, to create and establish a peculiarly American, to some extent isolationist, endeavor. That the seeds go back as far as Whitman does not alter the case. Under hegemonic conditions, what universalism or internationalism remains is internalized. Middle class English has long been sold out to the British. American English is collected from the regional fringes as well as the minorities (WCW: "What influence can Spanish have on us who speak a derivative of English in North America?"[9]). Blacks, Hispanics, Indians, then Italians, Germans, Portuguese, Poles — all purveyors of the American Grain. The act of collage continues; we piece together our culture with quotations: data quotations, language quotations ("Pin down an American and he utters a quotation" says Pound according to Kenner[10]). It is all one process. And to make sure that we can escape from the consequences of *continued* appropriation, we remain "open" — to the universe, to our fathers and mothers in poetry, to whatever grows out of the first line on our page (wherever we acquire the first line from, or the subsequent ones), forever and ever magnificently OPEN in contrast to the barbarous OTHERS who are forever CLOSED. Which is all reminiscent of another impossible ideal, from the early twentieth century European storehouse: the ideal of perpetual revolution.

It is this which seems to be so rarely looked at and considered: the political coincidence in time of American cultural hegemony and the appropriate techniques of "modernism" in the arts, including "postmodernism." I am far from decided on the issue, but it does seem to me to be an issue and I would like to see it discussed.

Charles Olson provides a fascinating "transitional" example. In his responsibility and commitment, his pedagogy, his effort at structure — even if he goes behind the twenty centuries to UR and SUMER — he is a "modernist." Yet, four years after reading through Butterick's *Guide to the Maximum Poems,* I remain dismayed by the *extent* to which these marvelous poems are made, without our initial knowledge, of texts and poems belonging to others.[11] Jed Rasula has recently introduced the concept of *composing* to define this process as cardinal in contemporary American poetics.[12] Mark Karlins has written a fine thesis on Olson, showing how such poetics can be seen as an act of abnegation: the ultimate subjugation of the tedious ego and the ultimate democratization of the world (problematic as this latter is for Olson) can both be justified by a poetics I would define as one of universal appropriation.[13] There is much in this to persuade me and there are times when I know that nothing is owned and that borrowing or outright stealing has been our mark of Cain from the beginning. Nevertheless, the magnitude and extensiveness of Olson's push in this direction continue to shock. There is another consideration. Those who have much may come with relative ease to the idea that owning nothing and using everything gives us the best of all worlds. Those who have little may find this idea less appealing . . . and less viable.

The "modernist" component in contemporary poetry is more traditional and more politically regressive, it appears, than the "postmodernist." On the other hand, this may be one of the illusions fostered by a "democratic" form of hegemony, in a word by liberal culture. At this time, it is hard to say.

Two contemporary concerns which address themselves to the theoretically-minded poet today — and again I use macrolabels — are "hermeticism" on the one hand, "primitivism" on the other. The former prolongs "modernist" interests in an elite-addressed content, usually connected to various esoteric traditions with universalistic applications. It also prolongs the "modernist" expectation of exegesis in that its poetries are rarely accessible even to the few, without a battery of critical reinforcements. In discussing "hermeticism," I would distinguish between masters of succeeding generations like H.D., Robert Duncan, and Kenneth Irby in whom esoteric interests are constitutive, the very breath of life, from the guru-hunters of all persuasions who adopt jargons from their latest enthusiasms and do little beyond muddying the flow of common discourse. That "hermeticism" here gives way to obscurantism is one illustration of the problematic aspects of pedagogy and transmission among poets working within a hegemonic context. The same distinctions would have to be made in regard to Buddhism's present hold on a large sector of American endeavor. In any event, "hermeticism" overall is mostly apolitical and therefore conservative in its effects if not in its intent. Collage and montage continue as important guiding compositional principles. Thus in our very schematic fashion here, I would tend to see "hermeticism" as being more "modernistically" than "postmodernistically" inclined.

"Primitivism" — as might be expected *a priori* from the relative simplicity of the poetries from which it derives its strengths and weaknesses — may be relatively more "postmodern" as a component of our silver decades. The father of American ethnopoetics, Jerome Rothenberg, leans towards an aspect of twentieth century European "modernism" often neglected or demeaned by most of our early American "modernists": Dada, Surrealism and the like. Ethnopoetics has inherited its internationalism from such movements; as far as the expectation of exegesis goes, it is clearly far, far less. To this extent, "primitivism" is far more liberal than "hermeticism" and, constitutively, far more open.[14]

Again, and far too schematically, "primitivism" is no doubt to be allied with the Beat wing of American confessionalism (as distinguished from its high-academic counterpart among the likes of Lowell, Berryman, Sexton, and Plath) and frequently moves away from narrow concerns with poetry alone to the wider, multi-media fields of the "counter-culture." It generates a poetry addressed to the people at large far more than any other faction yet considered in this piece.

In addition, there are signs of late that "primitivism" has been following surrealist precedents in calling more and more aspects of contemporary literature to shelter under its aegis. It would get rid of the term "postmodernism" altogether and gather under one banner many continuations of "modernism" from the surrealist and dada lineages especially. Specifically, Rothenberg, in a recent piece criticizing the revised Allen anthology, calls into play: Concrete and Visual Poetry, Fluxus, Intermedia, Chance Operations, The New Performance Poetry, The 2nd or 3rd Generation New York School, The New Black Poetry, Indian Poetry, Latino Poetry, the "Language" Poets, The Poem in Prose, The "New Sentence," as well as many individual poets for whom pigeonholes cannot be found. Rothenberg's stance, seen also in his *Symposium of the Whole* (with Diane Rothenberg) and the revised *Technicians of the Sacred* is admirable in its continued opposition to all forms of closure and all academic dictates as to the nature of the American canon.[15] Paradoxically, however, it remains open to question when studying hegemonic contexts. Paradoxically too, this enlargement of the "primitivist" impulse in the new, revised ethnopoetics may lead us away from non-elite addressed poetry. A digression on the "Language" poets may illustrate this.

These poets appear to be arguing the death of the "academic" versus "New American" controversy, to be replaced by decentralization of poetic activity in the U.S., an end to sexism, dispersion of poetic production/consumption among various "audience-communities" and the like.[16] For my part, I welcome the stress on mind, on intellect, as cardinal determinant of poetry-making and as attack on our culture's anti-intellectualism — even though I personally doubt that the group's products are intellectually or poetically stimulating. I welcome sophisticated forms of market analysis as one who has always believed that we badly need a sociology of readership, listenership, and aesthetic consumption. I welcome the politicization of poetics even if I find the Marxism of some of these writers derivative and smacking of the twenties and thirties rather than of our time — and their anthropology antediluvian. I agree with decentralization, desexism (if that is the word), and the identification and legitimation of audience-communities even if I do not believe that this will change the overall power-structure or validate Silliman's attacks on the "New Americans" for the crime of "commodity-fetishism." The poetry community — *pace* our dearest fantasies — is simply too *small;* the movement's books will fall prey to the same "fetishism" sooner rather than later.

My problem is that the theory of this "avant-garde" and of much of its experimentalism is almost invariably more interesting than the products: we *do* live in an age of conceptual art. In this case, and whatever the claims, the reduction of all this writing — except for a few notable exceptions (Clark Coolidge; Beverley Dahlen; Susan Howe; Leslie Scalapino; Michael Palmer; Michael Davidson among others) — to various degrees of non- or post-referentiality (under the touching but pathetic illusion that this can actually work as a tool against capitalism!) represents for me a relentlessly rehashed trivialization of the French neo-structuralist, neo-phenomenological, neo–Marxist, neo–Freudian intellectual life of the last twenty years or so. And it may yet manage to do to American poetry what that life did to much of French poetry: sterilize it and drive it nose-first hundreds of feet into the ground.

Returning to the theme of the "counter-culture": from the vantage point of the dull seventies and even duller eighties, the "counter-culture" of the sixties was a heroic epoch. It has left an enduring, often beautiful, often courageous mark on our material and spiritual cultures. Yet, the very ease and abruptness with which we passed from the sixties to these decades shows that its urge to make everything new and to give up all past solutions and panacea was such, when allied to its ignorance of, and frequent contempt for, history, as to make it resign any hopes it may have had for social effectiveness and continuity. With all its merits, the counter-culture could not, of and by itself, replace twenty centuries of human culture, organized, codified, and systematically handed down from one generation to another. In the end, it made America in many ways a better and more diversified place to live in. It did not destroy American political hegemony. And, while I am at the furthest remove from being a defender of the academy in its present form, academics know that it may well have damaged education so irreparably that the academy will have to be completely destroyed as it stands in order to survive at all in a rebuilt mode.

As one of the relaxing forces at work in our overall culture, the "counterculture" (others are the spread of general "education," the media, the ease with which we travel and so forth) would appear, in its ferocious overvaluation of the ego, to have abandoned collage. I wonder if this is the case. Where collage enters here, I believe, is in the all-pervading a-historicity of people content to write the same poetry over and over again because they do not know or care that it has been written before. Pound's injunction to make it new has vanished in an unparalleled drive towards a pluralism in poetic operations so extensive that the very possibility of any standard of judgement whatsoever seems to have been eliminated. What happens here, of course, is that you are quoting "history": what you ignore you are condemned, as the tag goes, to repeat. When every schoolboy can have, if he wishes, a poet's baton in his backpack; when — in relation to the market there is for the stuff, naturally — we are overproducing poetry to an unparalleled extent, how do we respond to the craft's immemorial respect for and evocation of order? It no longer seems possible and in this shipwreck might be read the death of the art.[17]

On the other hand, I have often been told — and I have told myself — that this is far too pessimistic a view. Also that it is totally wrongheaded. It may be that I do not understand the nature of "democracy" and totally fail to grasp the implications of general literacy (if indeed *literacy* it is!) for the arts in general and poetry in particular. This is what Williams appears to have been hinting at in linking his struggle to establish an American literature in the world with American poetry's "seeking a new adjustment to a new world — perhaps its final fruition depend(ing) on the entire social-democratic survival or collapse."[18] Whether this type of democracy will survive or collapse, however, is precisely what is being widely discussed beyond the borders of our poetry world. Despite all possible sympathy with Williams, questions remain as to *what* language (when so much language becomes debased among the media)?; *what* people (when it is so hard to identify a "people" now among the homogenized, consumerized mass)?; *what* democracy (when we have such a painful record of supporting so much non-democracy the moment we get out of our borders)?; *what* poetry (when twenty centuries of what is now being called "poetry of the word" [!!!] is giving place to "performance poetry," often no more than a morass of intimate theater and cabaret)?

I sometimes fantasize about what would happen if, one day, we were constrained to return to our own words: the words only we can invent, to which we have acquired a right by hard work. Or rather, combinations of words I suppose. It may be that thousands would heave sighs of relief. The Japanese, Indians, and Chinese would heave sighs of relief. So would the Hopi and Navajo, the Chicanos and the Puerto-Ricans, the Black musicians and the Polish Jews in our own land might heave sighs of relief. Our own ancestors and our dead father and mother poets might heave sighs of relief in their graves. What would be left of America when Americans had reconquered it?

In this situation, as a woman Asian-American poet and a woman Anglo-American poet pointed out to me the other night, my own experience of racism might seem to be a very mild one. Racism: labelling an individual as X or Y, pinning him down there, irrespective of his efforts and moves in any direction whatsoever. "British poet and will always remain so" is a form of racism. As the women said, almost *anything* this country had to offer might be worse. But is it not a woman who remains one of the most successful Britannic transplants in American letters? Ah, but Denise Levertov arrived, I believe, much earlier in life.

* * *

Instead of trying at all costs to achieve the "American," I believe we could live up to one aspect of our original mission by extending the rules of our own melting pot to the rest of the world: I mean the *original* rules. It does not seem to me that there is any real alternative to universalism, not once the planet has been SEEN from the outside. In this respect, poets like James, Pound, Conrad, Eliot, MacDiarmid, Auden, Levertov in "English" (but also Celan and Rilke; or Cesaire and Senghor in France, and many other examples) could be studied in the effort to find out whether poetry could survive beyond national "genetics." We could honor men like Kenneth Rexroth, our most universalist American master and, perhaps, our most neglected.[19] It may be, of course, that if we go too far beyond the national word, especially with our computers, our art, perhaps all arts as we know them, will cease and desist. But I have not yet given up the ghost in that direction.

Short of treating the contradictions as hideous instead of beautiful, I cannot, for myself, but take a both/and attitude to most of the diversification I have outlined here, rather than an either/or one.[20] It does not seem possible to me, in this complex time, for a poet to fulfill himself or herself without that extreme attention to language and the craft for which, for better or for worse, elite-addressed poetry is responsible. At the same time, the craft is mocked if it cannot also produce, perhaps in one product, perhaps in a variety of address, something available to whatever is left of the "average reader." I have tried to stress the perils both of "hermeticism" in which our everlasting battle for communication is often short-circuited and negated, as well as of "primitivism" with its promiscuous welcome to so much in the universe that any particular thing risks losing its uniqueness. I hope it is possible to go on from there, but that must be in the poetry that it is given me to make — if I am not rendered extinct by the state of publishing today, surely as disastrous and confused as any we have ever known.

To return to my initial point about English English and American English, Williams believed that the element of *change* within the former was the fertile one that Americans should follow. England had lost it: its poetry did not *use* the possibilities for change inherent in the language as much as it could have done. True or not, England becomes for Williams the stability/security pole so attractive to nostalgic Americans hankering after the delights of the Old World. The desire for security has to be resisted to face the NEW. To do that, the "very bone of English poems," the fixed foot would have to be sparagmatized.

The English father who refused to become an American citizen is a knot in Williams' being. His love for his father and his despair at his father not choosing the new is a vortex of contention and conflict, often evoked when Williams discusses the two languages and their poets. Then, note what happens. Pound is saved first as the first poet to write in the American idiom. Eliot becomes the great enemy. At a later date, Williams perceives that Eliot's childhood maintains him as an American . . . while Auden's keeps him English. Eliot climbs towards absolution, raised to the company of Pound, and Auden now bears the brunt of Williams' distaste.[21] And later still, Williams and his idiom gain some recognition. In some sense, Williams displaces the father and becomes a father himself. Around 1960, he is interviewed by William Sutton about Denise Levertov's "closeness [to him] in her way of writing":

> W.C.W.: Oh yes, very close. . . . She is from England. But she came to this country to seek a freer relationship to the line in our country, and she has adapted herself completely to our way of listening. She is a very interesting person to me. And she is a very skillful poet. She is half Welsh and half Jewish. That's a curious thing and must have its influence on the writing of her poetry. But she has rebelled from England and come to a freer place. Free construction of the line and has done very well at it. . . .
> I feel closer to her than to any of the modern poets.[22]

Astonishingly, Williams has acquired a daughter and she is British! (not quite English, note: Jewish and Celt)! The American idiom now has a daughter and the daughter comes from the Old World. The maturity of the "American Branch" has been established.

Williams eventually acknowledges that the American idiom has become hegemonic:

> Next we must establish in our minds the historical fact that the American Language invaded both English and French in the nineteenth century. . . .

The invasion, the modification of Yeats' corpus by the direct criticisms of Ezra Pound, Joyce (who never failed to read his Paris edition of the *Herald-Tribune* lest he miss the sayings of Andy Gump), Gertrude Stein, Hemingway, etc., etc. The thing to bear in mind is that it is the American language penetrating the European literary modes which should be studied.[23]

And in his description of Stieglitz, he recognizes the necessity for both branches: the "local effort" and "the forces from the outside":

> Stieglitz inaugurated an era based solidly on a correct understanding of the cultural relationships; but the difficulties he encountered both from within and without were colossal. He fought them clear-sightedly.
>
> The effect of his life and work has been to bend together and fuse, against whatever resistance, the split forces of the two necessary cultural groups: (i) the local effort, well understood in defined detail and (ii) the forces from the outside.[24]

Perhaps there is yet some hope that I can come home and all may be forgiven.

Notes

1. Nathaniel Tarn, "The Literate and the Literary: Notes on the Anthropological Discourse of Robert Redfield" in Sydel Silverman, *Totems and Teachers* (New York: Columbia University Press, 1981).

2. Quoted in Charles Tomlinson, *Some Americans: A Personal Record* (Berkeley: University of California Press, 1981), p. 67.

3. In *International Times* (London: no. 34, 1968). See also a "Nathaniel Tarn Symposium" in *Boundary 2* (IV, 1, 1975).

4. In *Io* (13, 1972–3), reprinted in Nathaniel Tarn and Janet Rodney, *Atitlan/Alashka* (Boulder: Brillig Works Press, 1979).

5. The Charles Olson-Robert Creeley *Correspondence* is in the course of publication by the Black Sparrow Press of Santa Barbara. Five volumes have appeared to date.

6. In *Contemporary Poets* (New York: St. Martin's Press, 1970). In the same entry, Martin Seymour-Smith writes "Tarn's poetry is . . . the most non-traditional and foreign-influenced of any British poet now writing."

7. Hugh Kenner, *The Pound Era* (Berkeley: University of California Press, 1971). For a recent statement on "postmodernism" see Burton Hatlen's review of the Allen-Butterick anthology in *Sagetrieb* (I, 2, Fall 1982).

8. William Carlos Williams, *Studiously Unprepared in Sulfur* (4, 1982), p. 31.

9. *Ibid.*, p. 28.

10. Hugh Kenner, *A Homemade World* (New York: Morrow, 1975), p. 84.

11. George Butterick, *A Guide to the Maximus Poems* (Berkeley: University of California Press, 1979).

12. Jed Rasula, "The Compost Library" in *Sagetrieb* (I, 2, Fall 1982).

13. Mark Karlins, "The Derivative Poetics of Charles Olson: A study of the *Maximus Poems*" (New Brunswick, Rutgers University Ph.D, 1982).

14. Nathaniel Tarn, "Dr. Jekyll the Anthropologist Emerges and Marches into

the Notebooks of Mr. Hyde the Poet," paper presented at the Symposium of the Whole Conference (Los Angeles, University of Southern California, 3.19.83). In Rothenberg & Rothenberg: *Symposium of the Whole,* University of California Press.

15. Jerome Rothenberg, "Keeping It Old: A Review of the New New American Poetry" in *Sulfur* (6, 1983). See also Jerome and Diane Rothenberg, *Symposium of the Whole* (Berkeley: University of California Press, 1983) and Jerome Rothenberg, *Technicians of the Sacred,* revised edition (Berkeley: University of California Press, 1983).

16. See Ron Silliman, "Realism" in *Ironwood* (X, 2, no. 20, Fall 1982). Note, in passing, that Silliman's identification of feminist culture as *the* major reason for change is queried, in the final piece of Silliman's *Ironwood* anthology by Kathleen Fraser identifying the movement as still male-dominated! For later, friendlier views on this see Tarn's contribution to Lee Bartlett's *Talking Poetry* (Albuquerque: University of New Mexico Press, 1987) and the symposium in *American Poetry,* IV, 2, 1987.

17. Nathaniel Tarn, "Proposal for an Order of Silence," in *Montemora* (5, 1979) and the symposium following this piece.

18. William Carlos Williams, "Studiously Unprepared" in *Sulfur* (4, 1982), p. 34.

19. See Eliot Weinberger, "Kenneth Rexroth 1905–1982" in *Sulfur* (5, 1982).

20. Nathaniel Tarn, "The Heraldic Vision: Some Cognitive Models for Comparative Aesthetics" in *Alcheringa* N.S. (II, 2, 1976); "Archaeology, Elegy, Architecture: A Poet's Program for Lyric" in *Sub-Stance* (28, 1981); "Fresh Frozen Fenix" in *New Literary History.*

21. William Carlos Williams, "The Poem as a Field of Action" in *Selected Essays* (New York, New Directions, 1969), pp. 287–289.

22. William Carlos Williams, *Interviews with William Carlos Williams* (New York: New Directions, 1976), p. 40.

23. *Ibid.,* p. 60.

24. William Carlos Williams, "The American Background" in *Selected Essays* (New York: New Directions, 1969), pp. 160–161.

A. Books, Pamphlets, Broadsides

A1   Old Savage / Young City   1964

(a) *First edition:*

Title: Nathaniel Tarn / OLD SAVAGE [slash] YOUNG CITY / [publisher's emblem] / Jonathan Cape / THIRTY BEDFORD SQUARE LONDON

Pagination: pp. [1–8] 9–28 [29–30] 31–36 [37–38] 39–64; 8 5/8″ × 5 7/8″; printed on wove paper.

Collation: pp. [1] title, [2] copyright, [3–4] contents, acknowledgements, [5] dedication, [6] blank, [7] half-title, [8] blank, 9–28 text, [29] half-title, [30] blank, 31–36 text, [37] half-title, [38] blank, 39–64 text.

Binding: Marbled brown paper over boards; spine black. Gold-stamped on spine: [publisher's emblem] OLD SAVAGE [slash] YOUNG CITY NATHANIEL TARN. White endpapers.

Dust jacket: Issued in brown dust jacket with photograph running from front to back, text in white. Front: Nathaniel / Tarn / OLD / SAVAGE / YOUNG / CITY. Back: no text. Spine: [publisher's emblem] Old Savage [slash] Young City Nathaniel Tarn. Front flyleaf: "OLD Savage [slash] YOUNG CITY / The world of Nathaniel Tarn is wide / and varied. He is cosmopolitan by / origin and education and has lived and / travelled extensively in Europe, Asia and / the Americas. His interests embrace / many sciences and most of the arts; his / work, slowly maturing, shows great / originality and depth of concern. / Poetry to Tarn is a religion of lan- / guage. In this discipline each poem / attempts to create a meaningful ritual / on behalf of an ancient, perennial world / which owns his main allegiance. This / world — in its primitives and ancient / peoples, its landscapes and animals, its / wise crafts — faces everywhere a hard / and stubborn death. The ritual's func- / tion is to keep alive its timeless rele- / vance to everything we do. / His poems, now making their first / appearance in book form, have already /

attracted attention by their vigorous / language and their remarkable individ- / uality of style. In 1963 he was awarded / a first GUINNESS PRIZE FOR POETRY at the / Cheltenham Festival." Back flyleaf: [list of other Cape books].

Publication: Published October, 1964, by Jonathan Cape, London, at 15s. Designed by the author. Printed by Ebenezer Baylis in Monotype Bodoni 11pt, 2pt leaded. Lithographed by Hawkwell Press.

Contents: 9 "Grief Is So Much a Now," 10 "Out of Sleep, Beyonded," 11 "To the Stillness of," 12 "Bring a Child Flowers," 13 "The Fineries," 14 "Head with Helmet," 15 "Ranger Spacecraft," 16 "Master Spy," 17 "Nomad," 18 "Last of the Chiefs," 19 "Prayer for Roses Newly Planted," 21 "Blackfly Melting," 22 "Some Peace from an Autumn Garden," 23 "For the Death of Anton Webern Particularly," 24 "The Eden Foxes," 25 "The Omen," 26 "The Cure," 27 "Not Asking the Way in a Park," 28 "Persephone's Down," 31 "Old Savage/Young City," 39 "Ely Cathedral," 40 "To Tell Andrea of the Ile de France," 42 "Remembering Benares," 44 "A Twilight for the Raj," 46 "The Moon in No," 47 "René Grousset Weeping at the Doors of the Shosoin," 48 "Adam Pacific," 49 "Portrait of a Modern Jew," 51 "The Wedding," 52 "Israel in the Park," 54 "Fountains Abbey Under Snow," 56 "The Delivery," 57 "A Rabbi's Dream," 58 "Simeon Bar Yohai," 59 "Abulafia at the Gates of Rome, A.D. 1280," 61 "The Master of the Name in His Privy, A.D. 1760," 62 "Noah on Ararat Again."

(b) *First American edition:*

As A1(a), save bound in green cloth; front: [publisher's emblem blindstamped]; spine: [gold-stamped] OLD SAVAGE [slash] YOUNG CITY [device] Nathaniel Tarn [publisher's emblem] Random House. Issued in dark green dust jacket; front: Nathaniel / Tarn / OLD / SAVAGE / YOUNG / CITY / *A Random House Book;* spine: as above; front endflap: revised text; back endflap: publisher's emblem and address. Published by Random House in April, 1965, at $4.00.

Note: I was doing my anthropological work in Burma in 1958 and 1959, returning to London in December of 1959. I had been worrying about whether I had a future as a poet or not. I had written my first poem at the age of five, then another batch at around thirteen. Sporadically through my college days, then in French during my years in Paris. The French poetry was a kind of experiment in going back to my "roots." But I became very involved in anthropology, most of which was written in English, and eventually French dropped out. From 1952 in Chicago until I came out of Burma I wrote again sporadically, this time in English, but nothing was really satisfactory. I felt that it was very necessary to have a socio-literary context, which I didn't have. I hankered after the

Tarn in Santiago Atitlán, in Principal *dress, 1953.*

World Fellowship of Buddhists Conference, Bangkok, 1958. Tarn seated at far right.

Parisian café as a model of the possibility of the availability of one writer to another.

While in Burma I had met a young lecturer, a Canadian poet who had previously lived in London for a few years. He had been involved with some English poets who had formed a meeting-ground called "The Group." This was basically a bunch of people surrounding Edward Lucie-Smith, meeting at his home every Friday night to discuss the poems of one particular person. It took this poet friend of mine about a year and a half or so to introduce me into that gathering. I didn't particularly share the "Little England" aesthetic of these people; in fact, I didn't share it at all. But I did appreciate the opportunity of meeting other writers and working in a collective context.

One of the poets in "The Group" was George MacBeth, who was also an influential program director at the BBC. The BBC came up with a proposal that one of "The Group" nights should be broadcast as a program, and I was chosen by Lucie-Smith as the poet. I did a set of the Hebraic poems which are contained in Old Savage/Young City. *Following, I sent the poems to a lot of people, including T.S. Eliot, though I knew his anti-semitic attitude might stand in the way of a reading. But I just sent them all over London. Things got rolling very fast, and poems started appearing here and there, mainly in places run by friends of "The Group."*

In 1963 I won the Guinness Prize for Poetry, which at that time was the highest prize you could win for poetry in the U.K. I went to the Cheltenham Festival to receive it, and at that point I met John Fowles, who was involved in the Festival. Fowles was published by Jonathan Cape, and he brought me to the attention of Tom Maschler there. I had a manuscript nearly ready. I went back to my college, King's College, Cambridge, and pretended to the Vice-Provost that I wanted to put together some articles in anthropology and sat for fifteen days in a room very close to my old room and worked on the manuscript day and night. Towards the end of this stay, I found E.M. Forster alone in the Senior Common Room, and felt a great need to confess what I had been doing. We had a very pleasant conversation about the whole thing. When I finished I took the manuscript to Maschler, who was very enthusiastic about it. He had had input from Fowles, and he probably showed it to his poetry advisor, William Plomer.

Maschler had known me in my anthropological identity some years before, and he was very delighted to discover that the author of this manuscript and the anthropologist were the same person. He asked me why I hadn't made myself known to him, and I told him that I wanted to make it just as a poet. I just didn't want to get published due to a previous identity.

At this point Cape had virtually no poetry program at all. I met Cape's son, who showed me the whole series of designs for old poetry books they'd done — very tastefully done, but very old-fashioned. I didn't like them at all, and asked that I be allowed to bring in other possibilities. I got together a whole portfolio of designs, mostly anthropological, and finally they took that great piece of Northwest Pacific Coast totem pole. I chose the colors also, and was very satisfied with the whole thing. When Random House published the book in America, however, for some ungodly reason they changed the colors and the thing became dreadful. But I always felt the Cape edition was lovely. And from that point on, until I actually joined Cape in 1967, I became one of Tom Maschler's principal poetry advisors, bringing in Charles Olson, Robert Duncan, and others.

A2   Thirteen to Bled   1965

Title:* * * / NATHANIEL TARN / THIRTEEN TO BLED / 1965 / * * *

Collation: pp. [1–14]; 8 ½" × 5 ½"; xeroxed.

Pagination: pp. [1] title, [2] blank, [3–12] text, [13] acknowledgements, copy number, [14] blank.

Binding: Issued without covers. Front: * * * / NATHANIEL TARN / THIRTEEN TO BLED / * * *. Back: [blank]. Stapled.

Publication: Published by the author in an edition of 75 numbered copies in 1965, none of which were for sale. An undetermined number of copies remained with top-edge uncut.

Contents: [3] "The Rights of Man," [4] "Baptizing Masai," [6] "Paolo's Dream," [8] "The Stain," [10] "The Life We Do Not Lead," [12] "The Winter Princess," [14] "In Such a Wind," [15] "The Satellite," [16] "Homing Bones," [18] "Dispersal," [19] "The Islands," [20] "Looking Back," [21] "Where Babylon Ends."

Note: Photocopied by the author for distribution by the author at the 1965 P.E.N. Conference at Bled.

       Thirteen to Bled *happened quite simply because I knew a man named Keith Botsford, who was both a novelist and a literary politician. He had persuaded P.E.N. to hold a rather elitistic meeting within the regular P.E.N. meeting at Bled that year at which people like Pablo Neruda and Charles Olson would be present. I felt the need to have something to hand out to people, so I xeroxed this little collection myself and gave it away at the conference. The primary thing about the conference that remains in my mind is taking Olson his first Cape contract for what would become Cape Goliard. It was for both* Maximus *and as much other work as Cape could get.*

A3   **Penguin Modern Poets 7**   1965

(a) *First edition:*

Title: Penguin Modern Poets / [rule] 7 [rule] / RICHARD MURPHY / JON SILKIN / NATHANIEL TARN / *Penguin Books*

Collation: [1–10], 11–39, [40–42] 43–74 [75–6] 77–111 [112]; 7 ¼" × 4 3/8"; printed on laid paper.

Pagination: [1] PENGUIN MODERN POETS 7 / D90 / [pub device]; [2] blank; [3] title; [4] copyright; [5–6] contents; [7] acknowledgements; [8] blank; [9] half-title; [10] blank; 11–39 text; [40] blank; [41] half-title; [42] blank; 43–73 text; 74 blank; [75] half-title; [76] blank; 77–[112] text.

Binding: Black wrappers with white design. Front: [in white: pub. emblem] PENGUIN MODERN POETS 7/ [in orange:] RICHARD MURPHY / JON SILKIN / NATHANIEL TARN / 3'6; Back: [in orange:] Published by Penguin Books / [in white: series statement] / *For copyright reasons this edition / is not for sale in the U.S.A.;* spine: [in white:] PENGUIN MODERN POETS 7 [in orange: Murphy Silkin Tarn [in white: pub. device] D90.

Publication: Published by Penguin Books in 1965 at 3'6.

Contents: 77 "Ely Cathedral," 78 "Grief Is So Much a Now," 79 "The Moon

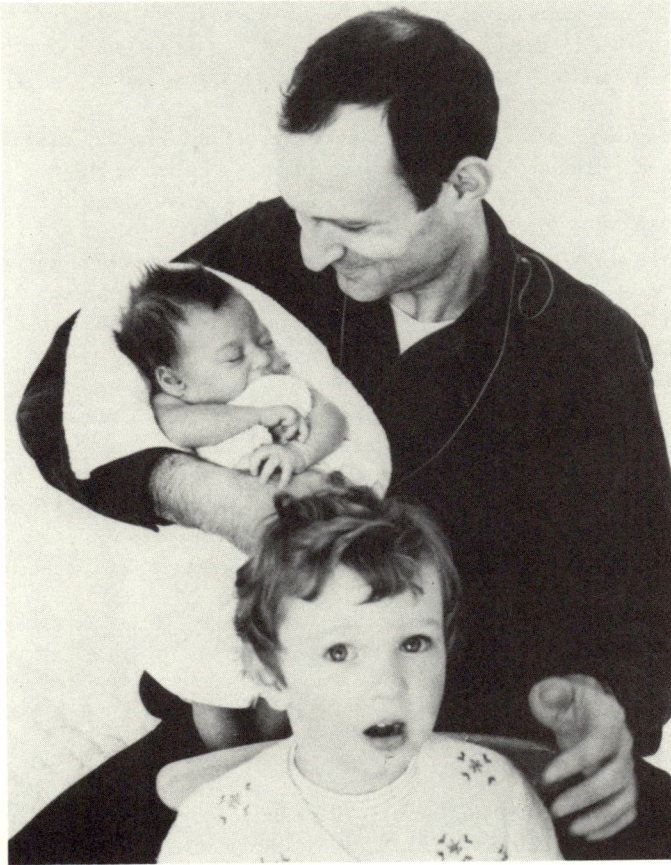

Tarn with his children, Andrea and Marc, in London, 1963.

in No," 80 "Ranger Spacecraft," 81 "For the Death of Anton Webern Particularly," 83 "The Eden Foxes," 84 "The Wedding," 85 "Nomad," 86 "Master
Spy," 87 "Last of the Chiefs," 89 "The Cure," 90 "Bring a Child Flowers,"
92 "The Delivery," 94 "Noah on Ararat Again," 97 "Old Savage/Young
City," 103 "The Rights of Man," 104 "Paolo's Dream," 106 "Baptizing Masai,"
108 "The Life We Do Not Lead," 109 "The Stain," 110 "Dispersal," 111 "Where
Babylon Ends."

(b) *Reprint edition:*

Reprinting identical as a save notation of reprint date (several) on [4]; front
cover: price removed; back cover: new statement concerning series printed
at top rather than bottom in white; [in white:] For copyright reasons this

edition is not for sale in the U.S.A. or Canada / [in orange:] United Kingdom 20p 4/- / Australia $0.65 / New Zealand $0.65 / South Africa RO.50 / [in white:] 140420908 [which also replaces D90 on spine].

Note: Unknown number of copies marked "proof only" issued in white wrappers. Front: Richard Murphy / Jon Silkin / Nathaniel Tarn / Penguin Modern Poets-7 / Penguin Books / Proof Only. Spine: PENGUIN MODERN POETS-7 PENGUIN. 7¾" × 5 7/8".

I met Tony Richardson, who was considered one of the most brilliant young editors in England, just after he got a good job at Penguin, one duty of which was running the Penguin Modern Poets series. We hit it off very well, and on the strength of my early work he decided to put me into the series. I think he asked me who I'd like to be grouped with; when the possibility of Jon Silkin came up I was very positive, though I had no particular feeling one way or the other about Richard Murphy. Even at the time I felt that it was too early for me to go into the series, but Tony's attitude was that one had to get in when one could, that one never knew when the whole thing was going to end. In fact, the series ran a very long time. The Penguin was used all over the British Commonwealth in education, so that for many years I was represented in places like New Zealand by only those early poems. The book was used in high schools. So it was a mixed blessing.

A4   **Where Babylon Ends**   1967

(a) *First edition:*

Title: [black and white photograph of eagle]; [verso: in blue:] Grossman Publishers in Association / with Cape Goliard London / New York 1968 / *Nathaniel Tarn;* [recto:] *Where Babylon Ends*

Collation: [1–44]; 9 ¾" × 6 ¾"; printed on laid paper, illustrations on heavy-stock onion paper.

Pagination: p. [1] half-title, p. [2] blank, p. [3] "TO MY WEST," pp. [4–5] title, p. [6] copyright, pp. [7–8] illustration, pp. [9–26] text, pp. [27–8] illustration, pp. [29–31] text, p. [32] blank, p. [33] half-title, glyph, p. [34] blank, pp. [35–41] text, p. [42] blank, p. [43] acknowledgements, "BY THE SAME AUTHOR," colophon, p. [44] blank.

Binding: Bound in ¾ green cloth over boards. Spine: yellow marbled paper over boards, gold-stamped: *Where Babylon Ends Nathaniel Tarn Cape Goliard [slash] Grossman.* Light green endpapers.

Dust jacket: Issued in stiff paper dust jacket, dark green. Front: [in yellow:]

Where / Babylon / Ends / [in black: illustration] / [in yellow:] *Nathaniel Tarn.*
Back: illustration. Spine: [in yellow:] *Where Babylon Ends Nathaniel Tarn*
Grossman [slash] Cape Goliard. Front flyleaf: [in yellow:] WHERE BABYLON
ENDS / by Nathaniel Tarn / [synopsis] / $4.00.

Publication: According to the colophon, "This first edition was Designed,
Printed & Published by Cape Goliard Press Ltd 10a Fairhazel Gardens, London N.W.6., March 1968, & consists of 2,700 copies: 2,000 soft cover, 700
case bound, of which 50 are signed & numbered by the author. 1,400 copies
of this edition have been printed for joint publication in the United States
by Richard Grossman Inc., New York. Printed in Great Britain." Published
at $4.00.

Contents: [9] "Where Babylon Ends," [11] "The Winter Princess," [12] "After
the Roaring Forties," [13] "A Head and a Lyre in Water," [15] "The Five
Senses," [18] "Markings," [20] "The Novice," [23] "For Mahler," [25] "Eagle
Hunt, Hidasta Indians, U.S.A.," [27–8] illustration, [29] "The Laurel
Tree," [35–42] "Projections for an Eagle Escaped in This City."

(b) *Paper edition:*   1968

As A4 (a), save issued in stiff paper wrappers; 9 ½" × 6 ½"; published at
$2.50.

(c) *English edition:*   1968

As A4 (a), save title paper verso: Cape Goliard / Nathaniel Tarn; published
at 21/-.

(d) *Limited edition:*   1968

As A4 (c), save signed and numbered by the author in black pen on title page
verso; published at £4.20.

Note: Where Babylon Ends *is a Cape Goliard title, and that is tied up with the whole*
Cape Goliard story, which is a complex one. What survives in my memory in a very
simplified form is this: I had been talking to Tom Maschler for some time about the way
in which I'd like to see poetry published at Cape. Essentially this had to do with an experi-
ment which put together the creative power of the little press and the distributional power
of a major publisher. I think I may have been the first to have that idea, but it came from
the fact that I'd already started to be influenced by American little presses. For instance,
I passed through San Francisco one night on the way to Hawaii and Japan in 1961, and
blindly picked up a number of books at City Lights, in fact forming a very good collection
of American first editions of that period. It turned out I had Olson, and Duncan, and
McClure, and so on.
    The point at which the Cape Goliard thing became a possibility was also the point

at which I was very seriously considering leaving anthropology altogether, leaving my post at the School of Oriental and African Studies and joining Cape as an editor. The heaviest workload of this arrangement was seen by Tom Maschler to be my editorship of something else — the Cape Editions. The change of jobs was of course very traumatic; that is, to give up my academic security and go into the business world was a difficult thing. I was Lecturer in Southeast Asian anthropology, and very possibly going to make Reader fairly soon. Under the English system this meant job security for life, and it was perhaps the best job of its kind in the world.

In any case, while discussion was going on I invited Tom to an exhibition of small press materials I had prepared, with the idea that he might choose what he liked best in terms of appearance. He picked out Auerhan on the one hand, and something called Goliard on the other. Now Goliard was a very small press in England which had been founded by Barry Hall and the poet Tom Raworth just a little while before, and they had just published Charles Olson's West. *There was also something by Raworth, and that was about it. I thought this was interesting because I had it in mind that Goliard would make a very good partner in this system, and what followed then was a series of very complex talks between Maschler and Hall. What emerged was the formation of a subsidiary company, Cape Goliard. The idea was that it would be set up with a press system of its own so that the two would not be tied together in terms of production, then the books would be marketed through Cape.*

At this initial phase, Tom Raworth decided that he didn't like the idea of working with a large publisher (though Cape wasn't all that large), and he and Barry Hall parted company. I was shocked by Raworth's departure, and very unhappy about it. I just couldn't see his arguments. The whole thing was an experiment in getting the kind of poetry I wanted off the ground in England, and it seemed to me that with very few compromises Raworth could have had a very good press to work with. This left Maschler, Hall, and me, though I was not there in a business capacity (to my regret) but rather as a kind of bridge editor who fundamentally belonged to Cape Editions. The general understanding here was that I would also be published by Cape Goliard, and thus Where Babylon Ends.

There was a slightly awkward situation throughout with Random House. When Tom published Old Savage/Young City *he said he wanted to sell it to an American publisher, and asked me who I'd like him to try. I knew something about the little presses — though I knew he wouldn't want to go with one of those — so I started looking up in a reference book larger publishers and it seemed to me that Random House was a major publisher. The fact that they did very little poetry save for W.H. Auden didn't sink in, so I suggested them. Very shortly afterward Tom told me that, believe it or not, he had Random House. My editor there was Nan Talese, and we got along very well. Tom had made a deal with Richard Grossman to take the Cape Goliard books in America, but because of my relationship with Nan* The Beautiful Contradictions *went to Random House.*

Opposite: A few London writers in Dulwich, 1963. From left: Zulfikar Ghose, B.S. Johnson, Edwin Brock, Alan Sillitoe, Martin Bax, B.C. Leale, Nathaniel Tarn.

A5   The Laurel Tree   1967

Broadside folio. 27" × 14". Printed on wove paper. Issued as part of Unicorn Folio, Series One, Number Four. Published in 1967 by The Unicorn Press in an edition of 325 copies, numbered on colophon page. Other broadsides in folio by Thomas Merton, John Haines, Robert Bly, Guillevic, Teo Savory, Eugen Gomringer, Boris Pasternak, Jaime Sabines, Lenore Marshall, and Wolfgang Roth. Typography by Alan Brilliant; printed by Noel Young.

A6   The Beautiful Contradictions   1969

(a) *First edition:*

Title: [verso, in gray:] CAPE GOLIARD PRESS LONDON / [recto: photograph] / [in blue:] NATHANIEL TARN / [running across verso and recto, in blue:] THE BEAUTIFUL CONTRADICTIONS

Collation: pp. [56]; 11" × 8 1/8"; printed on laid paper.

Pagination: pp. [1] blank, [2] illustration, [3] half-title, [4–5] title, [6] copyright, [7] epigraph, [8] blank, [9–15] text and illustrations, [16] illustration, [17–22] text and illustrations, [23] illustration, [24–35] text and illustrations, [48] blank, [49] half-title and illustration, [50] blank, [51–54] text, [55] colophon, [56] blank.

Binding: Issued in purple cloth over boards. Spine: [gold stamped:] THE BEAUTIFUL CONTRADICTIONS NATHANIEL TARN CAPE GOLIARD. Light purple endpapers.

Dust jacket: Issued in purple dust jacket. Front: [ornamental:] THE BEAUTI / FUL CONTRA / DICTIONS [in purple:] NATHANIEL / TARN. Back: [in purple:] 28s net UK only. Back: [in purple:] THE BEAUTIFUL CONTRADICTIONS NATHANIEL TARN CAPE GOLIARD. White flyleaves, no text.

Publication: Published by Cape Goliard Press, London, in April, 1969, at 28s. Graphics by Verifax.

Contents: [9] "The Beautiful Contradictions," [51] Notes.

(b) *First paper edition:*

As A6 (a), save issued in stiff wrappers, as dustjacket above, at 15s.

(c) *Limited edition:*

As A6 (a), save issued in purple tissue paper dust-jacket. Front: [in purple:] The Beautiful Contradictions / Nathaniel Tarn. Spine: THE BEAUTIFUL CONTRADICTIONS NATHANIEL TARN CAPE GOLIARD. Issued in purple paper covered stiff card slipcase. Published in an edition of 50 copies, signed and numbered in pen [2].

(d) *First American edition:*

As A6 (a), save front binding gold-stamped illustration; spine [in gold:] *THE BEAUTIFUL CONTRADICTIONS NATHANIEL TARN RANDOM HOUSE* [publisher's emblem]. Title: [verso, in black:] [publisher's emblem] RANDOM HOUSE NEW YORK]. No colophon. Designated "First American Edition," on copyright page. Published in 1970 by Random House.

(e) *Italian edition:*

Title: NATHANIEL / TARN / LE BELLE / CONTRADDIZIONI / a cure di Roberto Sanesi / [publisher's emblem] / MUNT PRESS

Collation: pp. [1–9] 10–91 [92] 93–99 [100] 101–105 [106] 107 [108–112]; 9 3/8" × 6 ¼"; printed on wove paper.

Pagination: pp. [1–2] blank, [3] half-title, [4] blank, [5] title, [6] copyright, [7] index, [8] blank, [9] half-title, 10–91 text, [92] blank, 93–99 text, [100] blank, 101–105 text, [106] blank, 107 text, [108] blank, [109] copyright, [110–112] blank.

Binding: Issued in stiff white paper wrappers, with flyleaves. Front: [in black:] NATHANIEL / TARN / [in brown: rule] / [in red: rule] / [in black:] LE BELLE / CONTRADDIZIONI / [publisher's emblem] / MUNT PRESS; back: [photograph of Tarn]; spine: [reading from foot to head:] [in black: publisher's emblem] / LE BELLE CONTRADDIZIONI / [in red: rule] / [in brown: rule] / NATHANIEL TARN. Front flyleaf: [Italian text]; back flyleaf: [other publications by Munt Press, price].

Publication: Published by Munt Press (Milan) in December, 1973, at 3.200 lire.

Contents: Dual-language text of *The Beautiful Contradictions,* with English facing Italian. Translation and afterword by Roberto Sanesi.

Tarn (center) with Elizabeth and John Fowles, Lime Regis, Dorset, 1965.

Note: The Beautiful Contradictions *is probably the book I'd choose to begin my opus with. The first two books were heavily influenced by what was going on in England at the time, while* Contradictions *begins to move out of that. Knowing that I was translating Neruda at the time, a number of people have talked about the Nerudan influence. Quite honestly, I don't think Neruda was a profound influence on my work, though of course his scope was an influence. The whole question of scope was very important to my trying to get out of the attitude of "Little Englandism" in "The Movement" and, later, "The Group."*

Pound was not a direct influence in this widening scope, though he was definitely in the background. He was just not easily available to poets writing in England at that time. Someone who was available as a liberating experience was Hugh MacDiarmid. At some stage during the composition of Contradictions, *a reading by MacDiarmid was announced in London, and I suddenly realized that I hadn't read him. I started right away, went to the reading, and undertook an epic venture to his home outside of Edinburgh. My reading convinced me that MacDiarmid was a giant on the British horizon. He belonged to the Celtic fringe, which I saw as more alive than the English. He was this huge mountain on which the little English sheep were grazing; they couldn't even see the mountain, it was so big. Neruda and Pound were there, of course, but it was MacDiarmid who gave me this feeling that there was nothing in the world that couldn't be discussed in poetic terms. It was above all that impetus which changed my breath line and*

enabled me to bring in my anthropological experience. My life got into Beautiful Contradictions *in a way that it hadn't in the previous books because of MacDiarmid's example. Duncan later remarked on that in a letter.*

   *A fair amount of the poem was written in a place in Wales. Maschler had a magnif-
icently isolated hillside Welsh cottage there; incidentally, it was the cottage at which
Ginsberg later wrote* Wales, A Visitation. *I think I was the first writer to occupy it
for any length of time — I'd go there for two or three weeks at a time, in absolute solitude.*

   Barry was very interested in Contradictions, *and especially interested in the
iconographic possibilities there. Again I trotted out vast files. Barry was a collagist, and
did the collages for the book. He worked with an absolutely unprecedented number of colors. He told me later that the illustrations were done in so many colors that the book could
never be reprinted, that it was outrageous to spend so much money in the first place, though
it was great fun! We had our little conspiracies, sometimes unknown to Cape itself.*

A7   October   1969

(a) *First edition:*

Title: [in red:] OCTOBER / [in black:] BY NATHANIEL TARN / *A Se-
quence of ten poems* [device] *followed by* / *Requiem Pro Duabus Filis Israel* / WITH
TWELVE DRAWINGS BY PAUL VAUGHAN / TRIGRAM PRESS
LONDON 1969

Collation: pp. [1–48]; 10″ × 7 ½″; printed on wove paper.

Pagination: pp. [1] blank, [2] illustration, [3] half-title, [4] illustration, [5]
title, [6] acknowledgements, [7] colophon, [8] contents, [9] blank, [10] illustration, [11–12] text, [13] illustration, [14] blank, [15–16] text, [17] illustration,
[18] blank, [19–20] text, [21] illustration, [22] blank, [23–24] text, [25] illustration, [26] blank, [27–28] text, [29] illustration, [30] blank, [31–32] text,
[33] illustration, [34] blank, [35–36] text, [37] illustration, [38] blank, [39–
41] text, [42] blank, [43] illustration, [44] blank, [45] colophon, [46] blank,
[47] illustration, [48] blank.

Binding: Bound in ivory covered boards. Spine: [silver-stamped:]
NATHANIEL TARN [slash] OCTOBER [slash] TRIGRAM PRESS
LONDON. Goldenrod endpapers.

Dust jacket: Issued in white dust jacket. Front: [in blue:] OCTOBER / [in
black:] poems by / Nathaniel Tarn / [multi-color illustration]. Back: [15 line
text] / 25s UK / TRIGRAM PRESS BOOKS ARE DISTRIBUTED BY:
/ *In the UK* Allison & Busby Ltd., 6A Noel Street, London WI / *In
the USA* The Bookman, 2243 San Felipe, Houston Texas 77019. Spine:

Tarn reading at the Nottingham Festival, 1966.

NATHANIEL TARN [slash] *OCTOBER* [slash] TRIGRAM PRESS
LONDON.

Publication: Published by Trigram Press (London) in summer, 1969, at 25s.

Contents: "October," "Requiem Pro Duabus Filis Israel."

(b) *First paper edition:*

As A7 (a), save issued in stiff white wrappers at 12s 6d. An undetermined
number of copies have two goldenrod endsheets bound in.

(c) *Limited edition:*

As A7 (a), save 100 copies have been hand-bound in red and white buckram,
signed and numbered in pen. Issued in glassine dj.

*Note: The three "pillars" I wanted to establish at Cape were Charles Olson, Louis Zukof-
sky, and Robert Duncan — not in any particular order as all three were equally important
to me. I had two rivals, it seemed to me. The first was Stuart Montgomery, whose*

Fulcrum Press had started before Cape Goliard. I had to fight him all the way and all over the world, particularly over Duncan. I had to persuade Duncan that Fulcrum could not handle him by itself, and eventually he decided on two publishers in England, Fulcrum and Cape. The Fulcrum effort was magnificent.

The other person who was doing very fine work was Asa Benveniste with his Trigram Press. He is an American expatriate and a fine poet, one who has remained in England all his life. At one point he asked to do a book of mine and the October suite was ready so I gave it to him. It turns out that it is probably the most beautiful of all my books. (I am not particularly happy about the looks of many of the later ones.) Benveniste had a great deal of control over his books. His stepson was the illustrator, and though I didn't select him I was very pleased with his work. We discussed doing another book together, but it turned out that I was too committed to Cape.

A8   October: The Silence   1970

Title: [in black:] NATHANIEL TARN / KUMI SUGAI / OCTOBER: THE SILENCE / *con due litografie* / [in red: publisher's emblem] [[in black:] M'ARTE EDIZIONI

Pagination: pp. [42]; 15 ½" × 11 ¾"; printed on wove paper.

Collation: pp. [1–4] blank, [5] half-title, [6] blank, [7] title, [8] copyright, [9] half-title, [10] blank, [11] text, [12–14] blank, [15] half-title, [16–17] text, [18] blank, [19] half-title, [20] blank, [21] illustration, [22–24] blank, [25] half-title, [26] blank], [27] illustration, [28–30] blank, [31] half-title, [32–33] text, illustrations, [34–40] blank, [41] colophon, [42] blank.

Binding: Lime green paper over white cloth boards. Spine: [in white:] TARN [slash] SUGAI. Unbound folio sheets laid into stiff white card folder, which is covered with lime green stiff paper, then folder laid into binding. Issued in lime green paper over card slipcase; front: [in white script:] Tarn [device] SUGAI.

Publication: Published in Milan in February, 1970, by M'Arte Edizioni in an edition of 130 copies: 5 lettered A through E containing an original Tarn manuscript; 5 lettered F through L containing an original Kumi Sugai lithograph; 30 numbered 1 through 30 containing an original lithograph; 76 numbered 31 through 106; and 14 designated I through XIV for particular individuals.

Contents: "October: The Silence" (English and Italian texts).

Note: All copies contain at least two signed Sugai lithographs; Tarn has signed and numbered the volume at [11–12], which is laid in as a broadside. Both lithographs and broadside are protected by single onion skin sheet. The volume is additionally numbered in pencil on colophon page.

Note: Somewhere along the line I met an Italian poet named Roberto Sanesi. There was a great deal of interest on his part in translating me, and later he translated The Beautiful Contradictions *into Italian. There were a number of spinoffs on the way to that, including this special edition. Sanesi had a relationship with various publishing firms in Italy, including contact with a man who ran an avant-garde art gallery called M'arte. Roberto translated "The Silence" from the* October *suite, then the great Italian art book making machine produced this item. To be honest, I was never terribly happy with it. While I wanted beautiful books, it seemed so coffee table and so art market that my own contribution seemed a little ludicrous. It was just too much of a collector's item. I had two copies, which fell apart completely; one was finally totally ruined through water damage.*

Interestingly, I actually had to go to Newark airport, open an enormous box in front of a customs officer, sign all the sheets, then close it and send it back. It was a very complicated scheme both to save me the trouble of going to Italy and to save customs hassles. It was all very strange.

A9   Concert   1970

Broadside. 18″ × 12″. Printed on light green wove paper. Published by The Unicorn Press as part of Unicorn Folio, Series Three, Number Two, *A British Folio,* edited by Edward Lucie-Smith. Issued in an edition of 375 copies, numbered on colophon page. Other contributors include Charles Tomlinson, Ted Hughes, Adrian Henri, George McBeth, Peter Porter, Brian Patten, Peter Redgrove, Lee Harwood, and Edward Lucie-Smith. Typography by Alan Brilliant, printed by Noel Young.

A10   A Nowhere for Vallejo   1971

(a) *First edition:*

Title: A NOWHERE FOR / VALLEJO / CHOICES / OCTOBER / [horizontal line] / *Nathaniel Tarn* / *Random House* [publisher's device] *New York*

Pagination: [i–x] [1–4] 5–52 [53–54] 55–70 [71–72] 73–77 [78–80] 81–94 [95–96] 97–99 [100–102]. 8 5/8″ × 5 ¾″. Printed on laid paper.

Collation: [i] blank, [ii] "Books by Nathaniel Tarn," [iii] half-title, [iv] blank, [v] title, [vi] copyright, acknowledgements, [vii] "South," [viii] blank, [ix] contents, [x] blank, [1] half-title, [2] blank, [3] epigraph, [4] blank, 5–52 text, [53] half-title, [54] blank, 55–70 text, [71] half-title, [72] blank, 73–77 text, [78] blank, [79] half-title, [80] blank, 81–94 text, [95] half-title, [96] blank, 97–99 text, [100] blank, [101] "About the Author," [102] blank.

Binding: Brown cloth over boards. Front, gold stamped, in rectangle: N/T. Spine, in rust: A NOWHERE FOR VALLEJO Nathaniel Tarn Random House. Tan endpapers.

Dust jacket: Issued in cream dust jacket. Front: [black and white photograph of NT in leaves; in center, cream rectangle, black border; in tan:] A / NOWHERE / FOR / VALLEJO / [in black:] New Poems by the author of / THE BEAUTIFUL CONTRADICTIONS / NATHANIEL / TARN. Back: [in black, at lower right:] 394–46289. Front flyleaf: [in black:] $6.50 / [in tan:] A / NOWHERE / FOR / VALLEJO / [in black:] NATHANIEL / TARN / [synopsis]; back flyleaf: [in black: synopsis continued] / [in tan:] Jacket design by Bob Giusti / Jacket photo by Ellen Levine / [publisher's address] / 4 [slant line] 71. Spine: [in tan:] A NOWHERE FOR VALLEJO [in black:] NATHANIEL TARN [in tan: publisher's emblem] Random House.

Publication: Published by Random House in 1971, at $6.50.

Contents: 5 "For a New Realism," 7 "A Nowhere for Vallejo," 51 "Afterword," 55 "Scorpions," 57 "Taking Leave," 59 "Apparition," 61 "Accidents," 63 "Choices," 65 "Swimmer," 67 "For Buffy Sainte-Marie," 69 "Aging Hands," 73 "The Great Odor of Summer," 81 "The Curtains," 83 "The Pictures," 85 "The Screens," 86 "The Dark Night," 88 "The Music," 89 "The Words," 90 "The Field of Merit," 91 "The Joining of Hands," 92 "The Residue," 93 "The Silence," 97 "Requiem Pro Duabus Filis Israel," [101] "About the Author."

(b) *First paper edition:*

As A10 (a), save 8 ¼" × 5 ½". Issued in stiff wrappers. Front: as dust jacket. Back: [in tan:] A / NOWHERE / FOR /VALLEJO / [in black:] NATHANIEL TARN / [synopsis] / Jacket design by Bob Giusti, Jacket photo by Ellen Levine / [in tan:] 394-70954-3. Spine: [in gray:] A NOWHERE FOR VALLEJO [in black:] NATHANIEL TARN [in gray: publisher's emblem] Random House.

(c) *First English edition:*

Title: A NOWHERE / FOR VALLEJO / [rule] / CHOICES / [rule] / OCTOBER / [rule] / *Nathaniel Tarn* / [publisher's emblem] / JONATHAN CAPE / THIRTY BEDFORD SQUARE LONDON.

Pagination, Collation, Contents as A10(a).

Binding: Black cloth over boards. Spine: [gold-stamped:] A NOWHERE
FOR VALLEJO [slash] NATHANIEL TARN [publisher's emblem].
White endpapers.

Dust jacket: Issued in dark orange dust jacket, with photograph of Peruvian
Ceramic running front to back in black. Front: [in white:] A Nowhere For
Vallejo / NATHANIEL TARN. Spine: [in white:] A Nowhere For Vallejo
NATHANIEL TARN [publisher's emblem]. White flyleaves, text in black;
front: [synopsis:] / 1.95 net / [rule] / IN UK ONLY; back: [blurbs from
reviews of previous books] / ISBN 0224007009 / Jacket design by M. Mohan
/ Jonathan Cape Ltd 1972.

Publication: Published May 1, 1972, by Jonathan Cape Ltd., at £1.95. Printed
in Great Britain by Fletcher and Son, Ltd., Norwich.

Note: The composition of A Nowhere For Vallejo *in Guatemala is explained in the
volume itself. As far as publication is concerned, the interesting thing is that I had
emigrated to America in 1970, and I suggested to Nan Talese that it now made sense
for my books to be published here first, then sold to Cape later if they were interested.
Thus* Vallejo *was the first of my books to be designed in America. I still kept a hand
in the design; I believe I came up with the idea for the jacket. I thought it might be time
for a portrait cover, and the photographer and I went out into Central Park and I buried
myself in that wall of ivy leaves. In looking through some archeological material, I came
across a beautiful piece of Peruvian Indian pottery which was in the museum of erotic
art in Lima. Among all the fucking imagery there was this very tender image of a couple
made up of a bird and a young woman sitting side by side. Cape took that as a jacket.*
    *Fairly early on in my dealings with Latin American poetry I realized that I was
more interested in Vallejo than Neruda, but the problem was that Clayton Eshleman had
devoted so much time and energy to Vallejo that it just didn't seem right to pursue that
project. But my interest in Vallejo came out in the very heavy role he played in this volume,
and the very heavy role his words play here. They are used as found poetry throughout
the book, and thus the book is perhaps as much a translation as an original poem.*

A11   For Buffy Sainte-Marie   1971

Broadside. 19″ × 12 ½″. Printed on wove paper; right edge deckled, outlined
in green with felt pen. Text in black, three linoleum block prints by Abbie
Reitz in grey. Published by The Unicorn Press in 1971 as Unicorn Broad-
sheet Series II, No. 2, in an edition of 375 copies.

Tarn in New York, 1967.

A12   Lyrics for the Bride of God: Section:
The Artemision   1973

Title: [in rust:] Lyrics for the Bride of God / Section: The Artemision / Nathaniel Tarn

Collation: [1–40]. 9″ × 6″. Printed on wove paper.

Pagination: [1] blank [2] "A Tree Book / Christopher's Press / 1973," [3] title [4] copyright [5] "in the vicinity of North" [6] blank [7] epigraphs [8] blank [9–36] text [37] afterword [38] blank [39] colophon [40] blank.

Binding: Issued in stiff tan wrappers, printing and artwork in black. Front: Lyrics for the Bride of God / Section: The Artemision / [photograph] / Nathaniel Tarn; back: [woodcut] / A Tree Book / Christopher's Press / $2.75; no printing on spine. Rust endpapers.

Publication: "Printed by Gary Albers at Christopher's Press Santa Barbara for Tree Books Bolinas, 1973," at $2.75.

Contents: [9–36] "The Artemision," [37] Afterword.

A13   The Persephones   1974

Title: [incorporated into design in green, vertical:] The Persephones /
Nathaniel Tarn / Sta Barbara 74

Collation: [1–24]; 9″ × 6″; printed on wove paper.

Pagination: [1] blank, [2] "Other Works," [3] title, [4] copyright, acknowledgements, [5–10] text, [11] illustration, [12–18] text, [19] illustration, [20–23]
text, [24] colophon.

Binding: Bound in stiff white wrappers, stapled. Cover: [in black, in script:]
The Persephones / [in green: illustration] / [in black, in script:] Nathaniel
.Tarn. Back: $2.75 Christopher's Books.

Publication: Published by Christopher's Books, May, 1974, as #6 in the "Hip-
Pocket Series," at $2.75. Printed by Gary Albers, designed by Melissa
Albers. Illustrations by Nathaniel Tarn.

Contents: [5–23] "The Persephones."

A14   Lyrics for the Bride of God   1975

(a) *First edition:*

Title: Lyrics / for the / BRIDE / of GOD / Nathaniel Tarn / A NEW DIREC-
TIONS BOOK

Collation: pp. [i–x] 1–148 [149–150]; 8 ¼″ × 5 ¼″; printed on wove paper.

Pagination: pp. [i] half-title, [ii] "Also By Nathaniel Tarn," [iii] title, [iv] copyright, [v] dedication, [vi] blank, [vii] contents, [viii] blank, [ix] half-title, [x]
blank, 1–148 text, [149–150] blank.

Binding: Bound in light brown cloth over boards. Spine: Nathaniel Tarn /
Lyrics for the / BRIDE OF GOD / NEW DIRECTIONS. White endpapers.

Dust jacket: Issued in white dust jacket, with black and grey photograph running from front through spine. Front: [in white:] Lyrics / for the / BRIDE
/ of GOD / [in black:] Nathaniel Tarn; back: [in black: list of New Directions
Books] / NEW DIRECTIONS 333 Sixth Avenue New York 10014; spine:
[in white:] Nathaniel Tarn / Lyrics for the / BRIDE of GOD / [in black:]
NEW DIRECTIONS. Flyleaves: front: Nathaniel Tarn / Lyrics for the /

BRIDE of GOD / [synopsis] / A NEW DIRECTIONS BOOK / $7.95 / ISBN: 0-8112-0565-7; back: [photograph] / [synopsis] / *Jacket illustration from a drawing* / *by Miquel Ocampo;* / *design by Gertrude Huston* / NEW DIRECTIONS / 333 Sixth Avenue, New York 10014.

Publication: Published by New Directions in 1975, at $7.95.

Contents: 1 "The Arrival," 3 "The Kitchen," 25 "The Artemision," 49 "The Invisible Bride," 81 "America," 111 "La Traviata," 143 "The Dictation."

(b) *First paper edition:*

As A14(a), save issued in stiff paper wrappers. Back: [synopsis]; spine: [adds NDP391 in black at foot]. Published at $3.75.

Note: The publication of Lyrics *by New Directions was generated by the departure of Nan Talese from Random House for Simon and Schuster. She wanted me to go along, but it seemed very clear to me that if Random House was doing very little poetry, Simon and Schuster was doing even less. I was afraid they might do one book or so, then everything would lapse. So I started looking around for another publisher.*

At one point, Kenneth Rexroth told me that he had talked to James Laughlin about publishing me, as well as Jerome Rothenberg. For some reason he had decided that we were the most promising poets of our generation. During this period I met Jerry in New York and told him that I thought Kenneth's trying to place me with New Directions would be like trying for the moon. I wrote to Laughlin, whom I had met in 1967, about the possibility of a book, and there ensued one of the legendary New Directions correspondences, in which J told me at great length of the financial impossibility of publishing new poetry in America under Nixon. But as he made it more and more difficult, I became more and more enthusiastic, and finally he agreed to doing the book. It seemed an incredible stroke of luck.

As usual I had a number of ideas for the jacket, but the designer insisted on the drawing that was used. I was unhappy about it, which may be what gave rise to a legend at New Directions that I'm difficult to work with. Anyway, the book eventually appeared and Helen Vendler murdered it in that omnibus review of over a dozen books. At the time the review didn't really mean anything to me save that Miss Vendler seemed inexplicably prudish as well as unduly personal. But it turned out to be the kiss of death, in spite of some excellent reviews, such as Hayden Carruth's.

A15   Poem Two (from: The Fire Poem)   1975

Title: POEM TWO FROM THE FIRE POEM / NATHANIEL TARN

Pagination: Printed as single sheet folded in half (6″ × 7″) on wove paper.

Collation: Front: text and illustration; back: colophon.

Binding: Single sheet folded in half. Light brown sheet glued over left edge, folded right to cover three quarters of printed sheet; right edge cut irregularly, traced with brown felt pen. Illustrated and hand-colored by Steve Wheatley.

Publication: Published by Caligula Books (Hounslow, Middlesex) in an edition of 200 numbered copies at 20p, as Miscellanea No. 4.

Contents: "Poem Two (from The Fire Poem)".

A16   Narrative of This Fall   1975

Title: [within red double rule ornamental frame, in black:] SPARROW 32 / [publisher's device in black at center of red ornamental leaf rule] / [in black:] "LIVING, I WANT TO DEPART TO WHERE I *AM*"—D.H. LAWRENCE / [red double rule, thick over thin] / [in black:] *Narrative of This Fall / by / Nathaniel Tarn / SPARROW appears monthly. It prints poetry, fiction, / essays, criticism, commentaries & reviews. Each issue / presents the work of a single author. The poet is prophet.* / BLACK SPARROW PRESS: May 1975.

Collation: [1–14]; 9 ¼" × 6"; printed on wove paper.

Pagination: [1] title [2] copyright [3–13] text [14] "Current Publications."

Binding: Issued in self-wrappers, stapled. Front: title; back: [within red double rule ornamental frame, in black:] description of "current publications," publisher's address, price.

Publication: Published by Black Sparrow Press, May 27, 1975, at $.50, in an edition of 1185 copies.

Contents: "Letter from Leningrad," "Antonin Artaud," "Sin Alternativa," "Narrative of This Fall."

A17   The House of Leaves   1976

(a) *First edition:*

Title: [enclosed in yellow rule rectangle, in brown:] NATHANIEL TARN / [yellow device] / [in green:] THE / HOUSE / OF / LEAVES / [beneath rectangle, in black:] *Santa Barbara / Black Sparrow Press / 1976*

Collation: pp. [1–10] 11–29 [30–32] 33–45 [46–48] 49–98 [99–100] 101–106 [107–108] 109–159 [160–163]; 9 ¼" × 6 ¼"; printed on wove paper.

Pagination: pp. [1] blank, [2] "Also by Nathaniel Tarn," [3] title, [4] copyright and acknowledgements, [5] dedication, [6] blank, [7–8] contents, [9] half-title, [10] blank, 11–29 text, [30] blank, [31] half-title, [32] blank, 33–45 text, [46] blank, [47] half-title, [48] blank, 49–98 text, [99] half-title, [100] blank, 101–106 text, [107] half-title, [108] blank, 109–159 text, [160] photograph of NT, [161] biographical statement, [162] blank, [163] colophon, [164] blank.

Binding: Half brown cloth, lime green paper over boards. Front: [vertical, in brown and gold: illustration] / [in brown:] NATHANIEL / TARN / [in green:] THE / HOUSE / OF / LEAVES. Back: blank. Spine: [lime green paper strip glued to spine; in green:] Nathaniel Tarn [in black: device] [in green:] THE HOUSE OF LEAVES. Green endpapers. False headband.

Dust jacket: Issued in clear glassine wrapper.

Publication: Published in an edition of 201 signed and numbered copies (1 of which is a "file copy") at $15.00 by Black Sparrow Press, July 27, 1976.

Contents: 11 "Letter from Leningrad to the Reason for Living," 15 "Food," 18 "René Magritte," 20 "Anton Bruckner," 23 "Antonin Artaud," 25 "After Jouve," 33 "The Roses of Guatemala," 35 "The Church, Santiago," 37 "Recipts," 39 "Desde Pachichyut," 49 "Wind River Ballad," 50 "Staying with the Laughlins," 52 "Connie Burrows," 55 "The Cranes," 57 "The Beaches," 59 "Thinking Her Name," 61 "Airline for Ariadne," 63 "First Cardinal," 66 "Her Lover, Mine," 67 "To Salamanca," 69 "The Thread As Before," 71 "The Seven Years," 73 "The Trains," 76 "Ladylike," 80 "The Opposing Coasts," 82 "Those in Washington," 84 "Sin Alternativa," 86 "Anniversary: In a Lyric's Margin," 88 "Olvido Inolvidable," 89 "Still Love, With Republic," 95 "Three Comings to the House of Leaves," 101 "To Meltzer at Bolinas," 109 "The Fire Poem," 116 "Between Delaware and Hudson," 132 "The College," 139 "Narrative of the Spiders," 144 "Narrative of This Fall," 150 "Narrative of the Readings in Chicago," 153 "Verse Letter to a Noble Person."

(b) *Limited edition:* As A17(a), save addition of unnumbered sheet [4a–b] on which Nathaniel Tarn has added an original drawing in pen (varies in each copy). Published in an edition of 26 copies lettered A–Z and signed, at $30.00. Additionally, though not noted in the colophon, 8 additional copies (1 "publisher's copy," 1 "printer's copy," 1 "binder's copy," 1 "file copy," and 4 "author's copies") were published.

(c) *Paper edition:* As A17(a), save published in stiff paper wrappers. Cover as above, save illustration continued on back. Published in an edition of 1512 copies at $4.00.

A18   Svairye   1976

Collation: Postcard; 6 ½" × 5 ½"; printed on stiff off-white card stock. Front: [inside decorative red borders, in gray: SVAIRYE / [text, 9 lines] / — Nathaniel Tarn. Back: [in black:] Membrane Press [slash] P.O. Box 11601 — Shorewood [slash] Milwaukee, Wisconsin [slash] 53211 / Copyright 1976 by Nathaniel Tarn.

Publication: Published by Membrane Press in 1976 at 25¢.

A19   The Microcosm   1977

(a) *First edition:*

Title: [in rust:] The Microcosm / Nathaniel Tarn / membrane press / 1977

Collation: pp. [i–ii] 1–25 [26]; 7 ½" × 5 1/8"; printed on "100% recycled" wove paper.

Pagination: pp. [i] title, [ii] acknowledgements, coyright, 1–25 text, [26] photograph.

Binding: Issued in stiff wrappers, decorated after a 15th century portolano map. Front: [in blue:] The Microcosm / Nathaniel Tarn. Back: [no text]. Stapled. White endpapers, with blue and rust design.

Publication: Published by Membrane Press in 1977, at $1.50.

Contents: 1 "The Light," 2 "The Creature," 3 "The Indecision," 4 "The Aura," 5 "Earth-Till," 6 "Provincial Morning," 7 "The Poppies," 8 "In the Scribner's Room, Princeton Library," 9 "American Ann," 10 "The Gate of Esperaunce," 11 "The Northern Lover," 12 "Girl in Soup—Kitchen," 13 "Girl From Another Tribe," 14 "Svairye," 15 "Standing Rock Sequence, The Dakotas," 20 "The Immigrant," 21 "Kadmon's Sister," 23 "On the Way to Green Mountain," 24 "Fossil Song," 25 "The Microcosm."

(b) *Limited edition:*

As A19(a), save issued in an edition of 26 copies lettered and signed in pen, [ii].

A20   The Ground of Our Great Admiration   1977

(a) *First edition:*

Title: From: ALASHKA / The Ground of / Our Great Admonition of Nature / *Nathaniel Tarn* / *Janet Rodney* / Permanent Press / London & New York / 1977

Collation: [1–24]; 8″ × 6″; printed on laid paper (Abbey Mills, Greenfield).

Pagination: [1–2] blank, [3] title, [4] copyright, [5–6] blank, [7–21] text, [22] blank, [23] colophon, [24] blank.

Binding: Issued in heavy stock purple wrappers, sewn with black thread. Image of mask running from front to back. Front: tarn [slash] rodney / from: alashka. Back: 80p / $1.75 / ISBN 0 905258 03 7.

Publication: Published in an edition of 300 copies in Winter, 1977, as number nine in the Permanent Press series by Robert Vas Dias, London and New York, at 80p and $1.75.

Contents: "The Ground of Our Great Admiration of Nature."

(b) *Limited edition:*

As A20(a), save wrappers folded over stiff black endpapers, issued in clear glassine jacket; back cover text transferred to rear endflap: 2 / $4 / ISBN 0 90528 03 7. Published in an edition of 50 copies numbered and signed on colophon page, at £2 and $4.00.

A21   Birdscapes, with Seaside   1978

Title: [within red double rule ornamental frame, in black:] SPARROW 67 / [publisher's device in black at center of red ornamental leaf rule] / [in black:] "LIVING, I WANT TO DEPART TO WHERE I *AM*" – D.H. LAWRENCE / [red double rule, thick over thin] / [in black:] *Birdscapes, with Seaside* / *by* / *Nathaniel Tarn* / *SPARROW appears monthly. It prints poetry, fiction, essays, criticism, commentaries & reviews. Each issue / presents the work of a single author. The poet is prophet.* / *BLACK SPARROW PRESS: APRIL 1978.*

Collation: [1–16]; 9 ¼″ × 6″; printed on wove paper.

Pagination: [1] title [2] dedication, epigraph, copyright [3–15] text [16] "Current Publications."

Binding: Issued in self-wrappers, stapled. Front: title; back: [within red double rule ornamental frame, in black:] description of "current publications," publisher's address, price.

Publication: Published by Black Sparrow Press, April 10, 1978, at $.75, in an edition of 1183 copies as Sparrow 67.

Contents: "Birdscapes, with Seaside."

Note: Sparrow 61–72 were bound into an "Autograph Edition" with separate titlepage; light brown label on front cover printed in red with single rule frame: SPARROW / 61–72 / Autographed edition / limited to 50 copies / Black Sparrow Press / Santa Barbara—1978. Published Oct. 13, 1978; 60 copies, 50 of which were for sale at $40.00. Each "sparrow" signed on title by author. An unsigned trade edition of bound first printings (120 copies) was issued simultaneously at $15.00.

A22   The Forest   1978

Title: [in black:] Janet Rodney [device] Nathaniel Tarn / [in red: rule] / [in green:] *The Forest,* / [in gray: illustration] / [in black:] in part, *from a much larger work entitled Alashka. / This part based on northwest pacific coast cultures / and their recorders. The four collage-illustrations / by John Digby. Published Thanksgiving 1978 by / The Perishable Press, Limited, Minor Confluence.*

Collation: pp. [i–iv] 1–5 [5a] 6–7 [7a] 8–11 [12–14]; 9 ¾" × 6 ¾"; printed on hand-made Fabriano Roma gray paper, bottom edge deckled.

Pagination: pp. [i] half-title, [ii] blank, [iii] title, [iv] blank, 1–5 text and illustration, [5a] illustration, 6–7 text, [7a] text, 8–11 text and illustration, [12] blank, [13] afterword, colophon, [14] blank.

Binding: Issued in plain grey wrappers, sewn.

Dust jacket: Grey dust jacket. Front: [in green] THE FOREST. Back: [no text].

Publication: Published by The Perishable Press, Lmtd., in an edition of 190 numbered copies, November 27, 1978.

Contents: 1 "The Forest," [13] Afterword.

Note: I met John Digby at "The Group." He probably stuck out as a sore thumb as much as I did. At the time he was the self-proclaimed pope of English surrealist poetry. He

Tarn (right) in Aspen, Colorado, with Toby Olson, 1967. (Photo by Paul Blackburn.)

was very lonely, a London Cockney who had been a zookeeper and was completely self-made, much like William Blake and Samuel Palmer. For about ten or fifteen years I was about his only literary friend. Eventually he came to the States, married a Long Island professor, and has lived on Long Island ever since. In time, though he kept writing poetry, he began to put energy into art, and has over the years become one of the great collagists of our time. He has written the authoritative book on the subject, The Collage Handbook, *and somehow came to the attention of Walter Hamady, who began using his work.*

I had been in touch with Hamady prior to The Forest. *I had probably met him through Toby Olson, who had worked with him. We got into a loose correspondence, and every now and again I would send him work. Eventually I sent him* The Forest *and he asked to do it. He asked me who I'd like for an artist, and knowing that he had a good relationship with Digby, I suggested him.*

A23   Atitlan / Alashka   1979

Title: [in black:] ATITLAN / [slash] / ALASHKA / Selected Poems / and Prose by / Nathaniel Tarn / New Poems by Nathaniel Tarn / & Janet Rodney / [publisher's emblem] / Brillig Works / Boulder [device] 1979.

Collation: [i–viii] [1–4] 5–10 [11–12] 13–17 [18–20] 21–31 [32–34] 35–47 [48–50] 51–54 [55–56] 57–95 [96–98] 99–104 [105–106] 107–148 [149–150] 151–156

[157–162] 163–183 [184–186] 187–210 [211–212] 213–262 [263–264] 265–299 [300–302] 303–308 [309–312]; 10″ × 7″; black endpapers.

Pagination: pp. [i] half-title, [ii] "Other Books," [iii] title, [iv] copyright, acknowledgements, [v–viii] contents, [1] half-title, [2] blank, [3] half-title, [4] blank, 5–10 text, [11] half-title, [12] text, 13–17 text, [18] blank, [19] half-title, [20] blank, 21–31 text, [32] blank, [33] half-title, [34] blank, 35–47 text, [48] blank, [49] half-title, [50] blank, 51–54 text, [55] half-title, [56] epigraph, 57–95 text, [96] blank, [97] half-title, [98] blank, 99–104 text, [105] half-title, [106] epigraph, 107–148 text, [149] half-title, [150] blank, 151– 156 text, [157] half-title, [158] acknowledgements, [159] text, [160] blank, [161] half-title, [162] blank, 163–183 text, [184] blank, [185] half-title, [186] blank, 187–210 text, [211] half-title, [212] blank, 213–262 text, [263] half-title, [264] blank, 265–299 text, [300] blank, [301] half-title, [302] blank, 303–308 text, [309] blank, [310] black and white photograph of Janet Rodney, with biography, [311] black and white photograph of Nathaniel Tarn, with biography, [312] colophon.

Binding: Issued in stiff red wrappers, with text in black. Front: [rectangle design of sun, embossed, gold and black] / ATITLAN [slash] ALASHKA / [on left:] Selected Poems / and Prose by / Nathaniel Tarn / [on right:] New Poems by / Nathaniel Tarn / & Janet Rodney / [below:] Including the complete BEAUTIFUL CONTRADICTIONS, / A NOWHERE FOR VALLEJO, CHOICES, OCTOBER, / and THE GREAT ODOR OF SUMMER. Back: Poetry / . . . we knew the immortal white of the place / is what we had failed to reach, / knowing instead our minds / in those of other men. / — ALASHKA / [publisher's emblem] / [rule] / Brillig Works / 1322 College Ave. / Boulder, Colo. 80302 / $8.95 ISBN 0-89681-001-1. Spine: ATITLAN [slash] ALASHKA TARN [slash] RODNEY-TARN / Brillig / Works.

Publication: Published in 1979 by Brillig Works in an edition of 1500 copies at $8.95. Designed by Ron Pyke, printed by Hoffman and Associates, Denver.

Contents: 5 "Old Savage/Young City," 13 "Projections for an Eagle Escaped in This City, March 1965," 21 "October," 35 "Choices," 51 "The Great Odor of Summer," 57 "The Beautiful Contradictions," 99 "Fragments from the Prayers," 107 "A Nowhere for Vallejo," 151 "Toward Any Geography/ Toward Any America Whatsoever," 163 "Cities," 187 "Out from Pennsylvania," 189 "Going Through the Gates," 194 "Western Rivers," 196 "Hamma Hamma City," 200 "Cities of the Dead," 202 "Terminal City," 203 "Blood Bank I," 205 "Blood Bank II," 207 "Gun Mouth," 209 "JR/NT: Each to the Other," 213 "Narrative of the Entrance to the Great North," 215 "July 4, 1976: Sevuokuk the Flight," 217 "The Lake," 217 "The Dream," 219 "The

Mountain," 220 "Bicentennial Ode," 221 "The First Men," 223 "The Ground of Our Great Admiration of Nature," 231 "Narrative of the Great Animal," 244 "Pendant to the Earth," 250 "Narrative of the Heartbeat," 253 "So Long, the Kenai," 257 "Letter from Homer," 259 "Three Poems," 265 "The Forest," 294 "Narrative/Invocation of, and to, the Race Klukwan," 303 "Perimeter," 303 "Marching Orders," 304 "What We Have Known As the Northwest Is the Southeast," 305 "Oregon Coast," 305 "Redwoods," 306 "Tactic," 307 "Home from the Nightless Summer."

Note: A few advance copies (undetermined number) were produced with earlier state wrappers, wherein the covers were flat rather than glossy red, and there was no golden figure in white rectangle. Further, following publication the publisher changed addresses. A number of copies have publisher's new address label pasted over printed address on back cover.

It seemed to me that having had the good fortune to have been published by New Directions, I shouldn't be too ambitious with them. I talked with Fred Martin, my ND editor, about this, and suggested that I take the weight off them by giving the next book to John Martin at Black Sparrow Press. Black Sparrow had been after me for years for a book. I had in mind a kind of alternation system. Everyone seemed to agree with this idea, and Black Sparrow thus took The House of Leaves.

The next book became something unusual, as I was travelling with another poet to Alaska. I'd been interested since my London days in the idea of a collaborative poetry to break down the capitalistic emphasis on one voice. It seemed to me that a man and a woman writing about one subject in a composite voice would be an interesting test. We both fully agreed on that. I sent some of this material to the New Directions Annual. No one really said anything, but I somehow felt there was some antagonism to my working with somebody else. In any case, in 1977 I received a letter from New Directions saying that they couldn't undertake the Alashka *project. When I returned from my trip I saw John Martin in San Francisco and suggested that book to him. He kept the book for a time, though finally took the position that he didn't believe in such collaborations, and in any case didn't understand how I could have put so much energy into a project with an unknown poet over three years. He rejected the book, but claimed he would do the very next book of my own. Soon after, I was giving a reading at Santa Barbara under the auspices of Kenneth Rexroth, and both John and his daughter were there. After the reading, she told her father that he was wrong, that she found the material very powerful. So I felt vindicated to some extent, though my situation vis à vis the publishing world had taken a very severe beating, for whatever reasons.*

A24   The Landsongs   1981

Title: NATHANIEL TARN / *FURTHER ANNOTATIONS FROM* / *BAJA CALIFORNIA:* / THE LAND SONGS / BLUE GUITAR BOOKS / PLYMOUTH / 1981

Collation: pp. [1–4] 5–12 [13–16]; 7 7/8″ × 5 ¼″; printed on wove paper.

Pagination: pp. [1] title, [2] copyright, [3] half-title, [4] blank, 5–12 text, [13–14] blank, [15] "Other Books by Nathaniel Tarn," [16] "Also Available from Shearsman/Blue Guitar Books."

Binding: Issued in tan wrappers. Front: NATHANIEL TARN / THE LANDSONGS / *BLUE GUITAR BOOKS.* Back: 0.80 / US $2 / HK $8 / ISBN 0 907562 01 9. Stapled.

Publication: Published by Blue Guitar Books/Shearsman (Plymouth, England) in 1981 for subscribers to Shearsman as part of the fourth issue of that magazine.

Contents: 5 "The Landsongs."

A25   Three Months in Which to Live   1982

(a) *Broadside:*

8 ½″ × 11″. Poem with illustration by N.T., printed in brown on cream cover stock. Printed and published by the author in an edition of fifty copies (number in pen in lower left corner), none of which were for sale.

(b) *Postcard:*

4″ × 5 7/8″. Identical to A25(a), save printed on white cover stock by the author in an edition of approximately 100 copies, unnumbered, none of which were for sale.

A26   Weekends in Mexico   1982

Title: WEEKENDS / IN MEXICO / Nathaniel Tarn / OXUS PRESS

Collation: pp. [1–12]; 7 7/8″ × 4 ¼″; printed on laid paper.

Pagination: pp. [1] title, [2] copyright, [3] dedication, [4] blank, [5–12] text.

Binding: Issued in stiff red wrappers. Photograph running from front to back. Front: WEEKENDS / IN MEXICO / Nathaniel Tarn. Back: [no text]. Black endpapers.

Publication: Published in 1982 by Oxus Press (London). Designed by Mary French.

Contents: [5] "A Departure," [6] "El Tepozteco," [7] "Origin of the Order of St. Domingo de Guzman, Oaxaca," [8] "Quertaro," [9] "San Xavier, Tepozotlan," [10] "The Rose from Ajusco," [12] "Union Mexicana de Organilleros."

A27   The Desert Mothers   1984

Title: [blue:] THE / DESERT / MOTHERS / [rust: design] / [red:] NATHANIEL TARN / [rust:] Salt-Works Press

Collation: [1–40]; 9″ × 6″; printed on Classic Laid paper.

Pagination: [1–2] blank [3] title [4] copyright [5] half-title, dedication [6] blank [7–19] text [20] blank [21] half-title [22] blank [23–38] text [39] blank [40] colophon.

Binding: Issued handsewn in brown wrappers (Beau Brilliant), with white thread. Front: printed as title. Blue (Grandee) endpapers.

Publication: Designed, handset, and printed at Salt-Works Press, 1984, in an edition of 400 copies, at $6.00.

Contents: 7 "Flight from the Mountaintop," 13 "The Bay Dies of Pollution & Decoys Rise in Price," 17 "The White Widow," 23 "Entering into This," 24 "Or that the President Would Abdicate," 26 "For the Rules of Flight," 28 "Death Fear—Yet of Another," 30 "Animal Bride," 32 "Peredur West," 34 "Rainer Werner Moves His Lady from Hollywood to Heaven."

A28   At the Western Gates   1985

[in rust: glyph] / [in black:] AT THE WESTERN GATES / Nathaniel Tarn / [in rust: publisher's emblem] / Tooth of Time / Books / 1985

Collation: pp. [i–vi] 1–14 [14a–b] 15–22 [22a–b] 23–30 [30a–b] 31–38 [38a–b] 39–68 [69–74]; 8 7/8″ × 5 7/8″; printed on wove paper.

Pagination: p. [i] title, p. [ii] acknowledgements, copyright, p. [iii] half-title, p. [iv] blank, p. [v] glyph, half-title, p. [vi] blank, pp. 1–14 text, p. [14a] glyph, half-title, p. [14b] blank, pp. 15–22 text, p. [22a] glyph, half-title, p. [22b] blank, pp. 23–30 text, p. [30a] glyph, half-title, p. [30b] blank, pp. 31–38 text, p. [38a] glyph, half-title, p. [38b] blank, pp. 39–68 text, p. [69] glyph, p. [70] "Other books by Nathaniel Tarn," p. [71] black and white photograph of N.T., biography, p. [72] blank, p. [73] colophon, p. [74] blank.

Binding: Issued in golden wrappers. Front: [in red and ivory: glyph] / [in red:] At the Western Gates / Nathaniel Tarn. Back: [in red:] A Tooth of Time Book [slash] $6 / [horizontal line] / [publisher's emblem]. Spine: [in red:] AT THE WESTERN GATES *Nathaniel Tarn* Tooth of Time. Golden endpapers.

Publication: Published by Tooth of Time Books in 1985 in an edition of 750 copies, at $6.00.

Contents: 1 "Journal of the Laguna de San Ignacio," 15 "Further Annotations from Baja California: The Land Songs," 23 "Jonah's Saddle," 31 "Palenque," 39 "North Rim."

Note: John Brandi asked me for an idea for a cover, and I suggested the glyph. Then he asked me to produce other glyphs for each section, and I did — a combination of Mayan glyphs and Tarn glyphs. He wasn't quite happy with the cover glyph and brought up the wonderful idea of having the glyph rain on the desert landscape. The way it ended up, I did the top part and he produced the bottom part.

I was very keen on the Cubist colors — white, black, gray, blue — but we didn't get very far. At one point I remembered that the colors I had used in making a crest as a child were yellow and red, and we decided to go with those colors. When the advance copies of the book arrived — no more than thirty of them — Brandi thought the red wasn't visible enough, so he had it changed to a lighter red.

A29   Children of a More Generous World   1986

Broadside. 12 3/8" × 7 ½". Poem printed in rust on laid paper; left and bottom edges deckled. Colophon: "Printed on the occasion of a reading at St. Mary le Bow, Durham, September 1986, by the North Gate Press, Durham." Edition of 50 copies, distributed free.

B. Items Edited, Translated, Introduced

B1   The Heights of Macchu Picchu   1966

(a) *First edition:*

Title: Pablo Neruda / The Heights of / Macchu Picchu / Translated by Nathaniel Tarn / *Preface by Robert Pring-Mill* / [publisher's emblem] / Jonathan Cape / Thirty Bedford Square / London

Pagination: pp. [1–6] 7–13 [14–15] 16–47 [48]; 8 ¾" × 6"; printed on wove paper.

Collation: pp. [1] half-title, [2] blank, [3] title, [4] copyright, [5] acknowledge-ments, [6] blank, 7–13 text, [14] blank, [15] half-title, 16–47 text, [48] pub-lisher's emblem.

Binding: Brown cloth over boards. Spine, gold-stamped: [publisher's emblem] THE HEIGHTS OF MACCHU PICCHU [3 rules] NERUDA [slash] TARN. White endpapers.

Dust jacket: Issued in black paper jacket, photograph on front. Front: [in white:] Pablo Neruda / The Heights of / Macchu Picchu / Translated by Nathaniel Tarn. Back: [no text]. Spine: [publisher's emblem] Neruda [slash] Tarn The Heights of Macchu Picchu. Flyleaves: [text in brown]; front: [synopsis]; back: [note on Neruda]. Designed by Peter Barber and Nathaniel Tarn. A few trial jackets (unknown number) fully illustrated in yellow and black, with text as above, flyleaf text in black, were printed; none for sale.

Publication: Published by Jonathan Cape in 1966 at 18s.

Contents: 7 Preface, 16 "The Heights of Macchu Picchu" (Spanish and English texts).

Note: An unknown number of copies issued in light green wrappers, with publisher's emblem in white, marked "Uncorrected Proof." As above, save front: THE HEIGHTS OF / MACCHU PICCHU / PABLO NERUDA / Uncorrected Proof; back: Ebenezer Baylis & Son, Ltd.; spine: THE HEIGHTS OF MACCHU PICCHU. [1] contains text of flyleaf copy; acknowledgements page numbered 5; no publisher's emblem on [48]. 8 3/8" × 5 ½". Tarn's copy marked "29th June."

(b) *First American edition:*

Title: [running across verso and recto:] *Alturas de Macchu Picchu* [slash] *Pablo Neruda* / THE HEIGHTS OF MACCHU PICCHU / *Translated by Nathaniel Tarn* / NEW YORK FARRAR, STRAUS & GIROUX / [publisher's emblem]

Pagination: pp. [i–iv] v [vi] vii–xix [xx] [1] 2–3 [4–5] 6–9 [10–11] 12–13 [14–15] 16–19 [20–21] 22–23 [24–25] 26–29 [30–31] 32–35 [36–37] 38–43 [44–45] 46–53 [54–55] 56–59 [60–61] 62–63 [64–65] 66–71 [72]; 8 ½" × 6 3/8"; printed on laid paper.

Collation: pp. [i] half-title, [ii–iii] title, [iv] copyright, v–[vi] note, vii–xix text, [xx] blank, [1] half-title, woodcut, 2–3 text [4] blank, [5] half-title, woodcut, 6–9 text, [10] blank, [11] half-title, woodcut, 12–13 text, [14] blank, [15] half-title, woodcut, 16–19 text, [20] blank, [21] half-title, woodcut, 22–23 text, [24] blank, [25] half-title, woodcut, 26–29 text, [30] blank, [31] half-title, woodcut, 32–35 text, [36] blank, [37] half-title, woodcut, 38–43 text, [44] blank, [45] half-title, woodcut, 46–53 text, [54] blank, [55] half-title, woodcut, 56–59 text, [60] blank, [61] half-title, woodcut, 62–63 text, [64] blank, [65] half-title, woodcut, 66–71 text, [72] blank.

Binding: Black cloth over boards. Spine: [in copper:] *Neruda* [slash] [in gold:] *The Heights of* Macchu Picchu [in copper:] *Farrar, Straus & Giroux.* Illustrated endpapers; second set of white endpapers.

Dust jacket: Issued in dust jacket, front illustrated in black, blue, and purple. Front: [in white:] *The Heights of* Macchu Picchu / *Pablo Neruda.* Spine: [in white:] *Neruda* [slash] *The Heights of* Macchu Picchu [in blue:] *Farrar, Straus & Giroux.* Back: [black text in white: list of Farrar, Straus & Giroux poetry books]. Flyleaves: [titles in black and blue, text in black]; front: [synopsis]; back: [note on Neruda].

Publication: Published by Farrar, Straus & Giroux in May, 1967, at $4.50.

Contents: As B1(a).

Tarn (left) with Pablo Neruda, International Poetry Festival, London, 1967.

(c) *First paper edition:*

As B1(b), save 8 ¼" × 6". Issued in paper wrappers. Front: Noonday 334 $1.95 added in white to upper left corner; back: titles in blue and black, text (from front flyleaf) in black; spine: [in white:] *Neruda* [slash] *The Heights of* Macchu Picchu [publisher's emblem] *Noonday N334*. Published in May, 1967, at $1.95.

B2   Selected Poems / Kenneth Patchen   1968

Title: SELECTED / POEMS / [rule] / KENNETH / PATCHEN / [publisher's emblem] / JONATHAN CAPE / THIRTY BEDFORD SQUARE / LONDON

Collation: pp. [i–v] vi–x [xi–xii] 13–35 [36–38] 39–70 [71–72] 73–82 [83–84] 85–88 [89–90] 91–124 [125–126] 127 [128–130] 131–135 [136–138] 139–156 [157–158] 159–167 [168–170] 171–180 [181–182] 183–191 [192]; 8 ¾" × 5 7/8"; printed on wove paper.

Pagination: pp. [i] half-title, [ii] blank, [iii] title, [iv] copyright, [v] dedication, vi note, vii–x contents, [xi]–191 text.

Binding: Bound in blue cloth over boards. Spine, gold-stamped: [publisher's emblem] SELECTED POEMS [three rules] KENNETH PATCHEN.

Dust jacket: Issued in blue illustrated dust jacket, text in white; front: Selected Poems / Kenneth Patchen; back: [no text]; spine: [publisher's emblem] Selected Poems Kenneth Patchen; front flyleaf: [synopsis]; back flyleaf: [note on Patchen].

Publication: Published by Jonathan Cape, London, June, 1968, at £2.75. Printed in England by Richard Clay, The Chaucer Press.

Contents: Selections from Kenneth Patchen's work, 1936–1954.

Note: Unknown number of copies marked "Uncorrected Proof"; issued in light green paper wrappers, decorated with publisher's emblem in white. Front: [in black:] SELECTED POEMS / KENNETH PATCHEN / Uncorrected Proof. Back: PRINTED IN GREAT BRITAIN / BY RICHARD CLAY (THE CHAUCER PRESS), LTD., / BUNGAY, SUFFOLK. Spine: SELECTED POEMS.

> *I was very fond of Patchen's work, especially the lyrical love poems. I was always on the lookout for titles for the Cape list, and one day I suggested a selected Patchen. There was already a New Directions selected Patchen, but I thought he was a fine enough poet to deserve another. Maschler wasn't very enthusiastic, but he let me have my head. My contribution as editor is pretty anonymous. I got hold of all of Patchen's books, though I did not consult the New Directions selected until I finished my own. When I compared the two afterwards I discovered that they overlapped by only a very few poems. Both Miriam and Kenneth Patchen were very happy with this selection.*

B3   Afrasian   1968

Special Issue of Afrasian magazine (number 1), devoted to poetry from Latin America, Africa, and the Middle East selected and introduced by Nathaniel Tarn, "Guest Editor." 10″ × 8″, [i–ii] 1–38pp. at 6s. Cover in black and white, stapled. Tarn contributes preface (1), as well as translations of Neruda's "Ars Poetica" (4), Neruda's "There's No Forgetting (Sonata)" (7), Neruda's "Alliance (Sonata)" (13), Pablo Armando Fernández' "Twelve" (17), Homero Aridjis' " 'La Difícil Ceremonia' " (18–9), and Fernández' "Birth of Eggo" (20) and "Surrender of Eshu" (21). Published by the School of Oriental and African Studies Students Union, University of London, at 6s.

B4   Con Cuba 1969

(a) *First edition:*

[running across recto and verso, decorative letters:] CON CUBA CON CUBA / AN
ANTHOLOGY OF CUBAN / POETRY OF THE LAST SIXTY / YEARS /
CAPE GOLIARD LONDON / EDITED BY NATHANIEL TARN

Collation: pp. [1–11] 12–144; 10″ × 6 ¾″; printed on laid paper.

Pagination: pp. [1–2] blank, [3] half-title, [4–5] title, [6] copyright, [7–9] contents, [10] blank, [11] preface, 12–139 text, 140 blank, 141–42 sources, 143 colophon, 144 blank.

Binding: Bound in red cloth over boards. Spine: [gold-stamped, decorative letters:] CON CUBA Edited by NATHANIEL TARN Cape Goliard. Dark green endpapers.

Dust jacket: Issued in white dust jacket. Front: [in red and gray: CON [in blue and gray:] CUBA / [illustration in gray]; back: [in gray:] An Anthology of Cuban Poetry / Of the Last Sixty Years / [in red and gray:] EDITED BY NATHANIEL TARN / [in blue and gray:] THE POETS / [in gray:] Rafael Alcides Orlando Alomá / Miguel Barnet Victor Casaus / Eliseo Diego Froilán Escobar / David Fernández Samuel Feijóo / Pablo Armando Fernández / Lina De Feria Felix Guerra / José Lezama Lima Eduardo Lolo / César López Nancy Morejón / Fayad Jamís Luis Marré / Gerardo Fulleda León Isel Rivero / Manuel Díaz Martínez / Luis Rogelio Nogueras / Belkis Cuza Malé Herberto Padilla / Felix Pita Rodríguez Cinto Vitier / Pedro De Oraá Luis Suardiaz / Fina García Marruz / Roberto Fernández Retamar / Guillermo Rodríguez Rivera / [in red and gray:] TRANSLATED BY / [in gray:] Elinor Randall Margaret Randall / Tom Raworth Nathaniel Tarn / Stephen Schwartz Tim Reynolds / Adrian Mitchell David Ossman / Donald Gardner Carl Hagen / [in red:] 30 SHILLINGS NET. U.K. ONLY / [in gray:] Lionel Kearns Anthony Kerrigan; spine: [in gray and blue:] CON CUBA [in gray:] Edited by [in gray and blue:] NATHANIEL TARN [in gray:] Cape Goliard.

Publication: Published in 1969 by Cape Goliard Press at 30s; printed in Great Britain.

Contents: [11] preface by N.T., 16–21 José Lezama Lima [trans. N.T.], 26–9 Eliseo Diego [trans. N.T.], 34–7 Cintio Vitier [trans. N.T.], 44–7 Pablo Armando Fernández [trans. by N.T.], 60–3 Roberto Fernández Retamar [trans. N.T.], 112–13 Belkis Cuza Malé [trans. N.T.], 114–15 Guillermo

Rodríguez Rivera [trans. N.T.], 124–25 Nancy Morejón [trans. N.T.].

(b) *Paper edition:*

As B4(a), save issued in stiff wrappers, with two green endpapers front and rear. 9 ¾″ × 6 ½″.

B5   Victor Segalen: Stelae   1969

(a) *First edition:*

Title: [in black:] VICTOR SEGALEN / [in green:] Stelae / [in black:] TRANSLATED FROM THE FRENCH BY / NATHANIEL TARN / [in green:] device / [in black:] UNICORN PRESS

Pagination: pp. [1–12] 13–21 [22–24] 25–26 [27–28] 29–38 [39–40] 41–43 [44–46] 47–50 [51–52] 53–58 [59–61] 62–93 [94] 95 [96]; 7 ¾″ × 5 5/8″; printed on wove paper.

Collation: pp. [1] illustration, [2] photograph, [3] title, [4] copyright, [5] text, [6–7] contents, [8–9] introduction, [10] blank, [11] half-title, [12] blank, 13–21 text, [22] blank, [23] half-title, [24] blank, 25–26 text, [27] half-title, [28] blank, 29–38 text, [39] half-title, [40] blank, 41–43 text, [44] blank, [45] half-title, [46] blank, 47–50 text, [51] half-title, [52] blank, 53–58 text, [59] photograph, [60] photograph, [61 contents], 62–93 text, [94] blank, 95 note, [96] blank.

Binding: Bound in light green cloth over boards. Front: [white label pasted on, black rule border, in green:] SEGALEN / [in black: rule] / [in green:] UNICORN FRENCH SERIES. Back: [no text]. Spine: [white label pasted on:] SEGALEN [device] *Unicorn French Series.* White endpapers.

Publication: Published by Unicorn Press in 1969, at $6.00, as volume nine in the Unicorn French Series, Teo Savory, editor. Printed by Noel Young, designed by Alan Brilliant. Calligraphy by Donald Rojo.

Contents: [8–9] Introduction, 13–58 Segalen's *Stelae,* translated by N.T., 62–93 French text.

(b) *First paper edition:*

As B5(a), save issued in decorated light green wrappers. Spine: [printed,

Tarn (far left) at the Cuban Cultural Congress, Havana, 1968. Arnold Wesker is seated to Tarn's immediate left.

in green:] SEGALEN [device] *Unicorn French Series.* 7 ½ " × 5 ½"; light green endpapers. Published at $3.00.

Note: I was always on the lookout for worthwhile things to do in translation, and I was interested in Segalen because he was a poet on the one hand and an archeologist on the other. He had worked in China, was the first man to get to Gauguin's hut just after the artist's death, had been a friend of Debussy, Claudel, and many others. And it turned out that he hadn't been translated into English before. I bought a very large collection of his in Paris, and discovered that a lot of the work was in rhymed verse, which I didn't want to tangle with. The most immediately available thing for me then became Stelae.

The Unicorn book had a strange history. At the start it sold very well, though it was never reviewed. Then suddenly there was a period of a couple years in which I just simply did not know what happened to it. I discovered by chance that there had been some kind of fight between the publisher and a bookstore, and somehow the book became imprisoned. Eventually, all the copies went into storage somewhere, though finally they emerged for distribution and are available again.

Alcheringa *meeting, Santa Fe, 1970. From left: Larry Bird, Tarn, Jerome Rothenberg, Harold Littlebird.*

B6   Pablo Neruda: Selected Poems   1970

(a) *First edition:*

Title: Pablo Neruda / SELECTED POEMS / EDITED BY NATHANIEL TARN / Translated by ANTHONY KERRIGAN, W.S. MERWIN, / ALASTAIR REID and NATHANIEL TARN / [publisher's emblem] / JONATHAN CAPE / THIRTY BEDFORD SQUARE LONDON

Pagination: pp. [1–15] 16–35 [36–37] 38–85 [86–87] 88–123 [124–125] 126–161 [162–163] 164–277 [278–279] 280–343 [344–345] 346–349 [350–351] 352–407 [408–409] 410–419 [420–421] 422–425 [426–427] 428–453 [454–455] 456–485 [486– 487] 488–491 [492–493] 494–501 [502–504]; 8 ¾″ × 5 7/8″; printed on laid paper.

Collation: pp. [1] half-title, [2] blank, [3] title, [4] copyright, [5–7] Editor's Foreword, [8] blank, [9–13] contents, [14] blank, [15] half-title, 16–35 text, [36] blank, [37] half-title, 38–85 text, [86] blank, [87] half-title, 88–123 text, [124] blank, [125] half-title, 126–161 text, [162] blank, [163] half-title, 164–277 text, [278] blank, [279] half-title, 280–343 text, [344] blank, [345] half-title, 346–349 text, [350] blank, [351] half-title, 352–407 text, [408] blank, [409] half-title, 410–419 text, [420] blank, [421] half-title, 422–425 text, [426] blank, [427] half-title, 428–453 text, [454] blank, [455] half-title, 456–485 text, [486] blank, [487] half-title, 488–491 text, [492] blank, [493] half-title, 494–501 text, [502–504] blank.

Binding: Bound in blue and white cloth over boards. Spine, gold-stamped: SELECTED / POEMS / PABLO / NERUDA / [rule] / EDITED BY / NATHANIEL TARN / TRANSLATORS / ANTHONY KERRIGAN / W.S. MERWIN / ALASTAIR REID / NATHANIEL TARN / [publisher's emblem]. White endpapers.

Dust jacket: Issued in purple dust jacket with illustration in black, running from front to back. Front: [in white:] Selected Poems / Pablo Neruda / Edited by Nathaniel Tarn / Translators: ANTHONY KERRIGAN / W.S. MERWIN, ALASTAIR REID / NATHANIEL TARN. Back: no text. Spine: [in white:] Selected / Poems / Pablo / Neruda / Edited by / Nathaniel Tarn / Translators: / ANTHONY KERRIGAN / W.S. MERWIN / ALASTAIR REID / NATHANIEL TARN / [publisher's emblem]. White flyleaves, text in black; front: [synopsis]; back: [biographical note on Neruda].

Publication: Published by Jonathan Cape in 1970, at £3.25. Printed by Richard Clay, The Chaucer Press, Suffolk.

Contents: [5-7] Editor's Foreword, 16-501 Bilingual text, with translations by Anthony Kerrigan, W.S. Merwin, Alastair Reid, and Nathaniel Tarn.

(b) *First American edition:*

Title: Pablo / Neruda / [rule] / SELECTED / POEMS / A BILINGUAL EDITION / Edited by NATHANIEL TARN / Translated by ANTHONY KERRIGAN, / W.S. MERWIN, ALASTAIR REID / and NATHANIEL TARN / DELACORTE PRESS [slash] SEYMOUR LAWRENCE

Pagination: As B6(a), save 503-505 [506] 507-509 [510-512]; 9 ¼" × 6 ¼".

Collation: As B6(a), save pp. 503-505 English index of first lines, [506] blank, 507-509 Spanish index of first lines, [510-512] blank.

Binding: Bound in light and dark brown over boards. Front: [gold-stamped:] *Pablo / Neruda.* Spine: [gold-stamped:] PABLO / NERUDA / [ornate device] / SELECTED / POEMS / EDITED BY / NATHANIEL TARN / TRANS-LATED BY / ANTHONY KERRIGAN / W.S. MERWIN / ALASTAIR REID / NATHANIEL TARN / DELACORTE PRESS. Purple endpapers.

Dust jacket: Issued in purple dust jacket. Front: [in red:] Winner of the 1971 Nobel Prize for Literature / PABLO / NERUDA / [in purple: ornate device] / [in brown:] SELECTED POEMS / A Bilingual Edition / [in red:] Edited by Nathaniel Tarn / [in brown:] TRANSLATORS / [in red: rule] / [in brown:] Anthony Kerrigan / W.S. Merwin / Alastair Reid / Nathaniel Tarn. Back: [photograph] / [in purple:] HANS EHRMANN. Spine: [in red:] PABLO / NERUDA [in red: rule] / [in brown:] SELECTED POEMS / [in red: rule] / [in brown:] Edited by Nathaniel Tarn / TRANSLATORS / [in red: rule] / [in brown:] Anthony Kerrigan / W.S. Merwin / Alastair Reid / Nathaniel Tarn / [in purple: publisher's emblem] / [in brown:] Delacorte Press. Flyleaves: [titles in red, purple, brown, and black]; [synopsis in black].

Publication: Published by Dell Publishing Company, Inc. in 1972, at $12.50. Copyright page designates "First American Edition."

Contents: As B6(a).

(c) *First paper edition:*

As B6(b), save issued in stiff paper wrappers. Front adds in brown at head: DELTA [publisher's emblem] $2.95; back: [blurbs from reviews, biographical note]; spine: [adds publisher's emblem in brown at head], 440-07879-295 [at foot]. No endpapers. Copyright page designates "First Delta Printing — February 1973." Published at $2.95.

Note: Not long after I started advising Cape in 1964, Tom Maschler signed Neruda for some kind of translation, some kind of substantial selected poems. Because we were close at the time, I heard about it right away and asked to participate; Maschler more or less gave me the whole job. It became clear to me very soon that there was a substantial number of people already working on Neruda, and there was something rather presumptious about trying to do the whole project myself. On the other hand, I wanted to avoid the business of simply pulling together all the translations that had ever been done, of doing a selected or collected Neruda with dozens and dozens of translators. I finally hit upon a middle way — working with three other translators whose work was not yet published. Thus, for example, Robert Bly would not have been a candidate because he had already published his Neruda translations, while W.S. Merwin, Anthony Kerrigan, and Alastair Reid would.

I took Neruda's most important poems, The Heights of Macchu Picchu, *and translated the whole of it as a beginning towards this task as I was writing to the others and arranging the selected poems. There was a Neruda scholar at Oxford, Robert Pring-Mill, with whom I worked in very close collaboration. We spent enormously long sessions at his college in Oxford wherein he went over every single page, sentence, word, letter, punctuation mark. The worksheets for the project are in something like fifteen different colors of ink. While I greatly valued this collaboration, I emerged so exhausted and constrained that the later translations were not submitted to Pring-Mill. This later lack of vetting did turn out to be a problem as a number of people pointed out various errors.*

The actual selections for the Selected Poems *didn't turn out to be as difficult to make as I thought they would be. Each translator had interest in different areas of*

Neruda's work in advance: Reid was interested in the later part, Kerrigan in the Canto General *period, Merwin and I in the* Residencia *period. Because I was in touch with Neruda, who came to London on a number of occasions, I thought it best to let him make the actual selections, which he did. At that particular time, for his own reasons, he was not all that keen on including too many of the political poems. He visited me at my home a few times, and I was planning to travel to Chile to see him when the coup overthrowing Allende occurred, and he died.*

B7   Pablo Neruda / Selected Poems   1975

Title: Selected Poems / Pablo Neruda / Edited by Nathaniel Tarn / Translated by Anthony Kerrigan, / W.S. Merwin, / Alastair Reid / and Nathaniel Tarn / with an Introduction by / Jean Franco / [publisher's emblem] Penguin Books

Pagination: pp. [1–5] 6–9 [10] 11–23 [24–25] 26–33 [34–35] 36–55 [56–57] 58–75 [76–77] 78–109 [110–111] 112–157 [158–159] 160–169 [170–171] 172–187 [188–189] 190–193 [194–195] 196–199 [200–201] 202–213 [214–215] 216–225 [226–227] 228–229 [230–231] 232–237 [234–236]; 7 ¾″ × 5″; printed on wove paper.

Collation: pp. [1] biograpical note, [2] blank, [3] title, [4] copyright, [5] blank, 6–9 contents, [10] blank, 11–12 Editor's Foreword, 13–23 Introduction, [24] blank, [25] half-title, 26–33 text, [34] blank, [35] half-title, 36–55 text, [56] blank, [57] half-title, 58–75 text, [76] blank, [77] half-title, 78–109 text, [110] blank, [111] half-title, 112–157 text, [158] blank, [159] half-title, 160–169 text, [170] blank, [171] half-title, 172–187 text, [188] blank, [189] half-title, 190–193 text, [194] blank, [195] half-title, 196–199 text, [200] blank, [201] half-title, 202–213 text, [214] blank, [215] half-title, 216–225 text, [226] blank, [227] half-title, 228–229 text, [230] blank, [231] half-title, 232–237 text, [238] blank, [239] ad, [240] blank.

Binding: Issued in stiff yellow wrappers. Front [over brown photograph of Neruda; in black:] Pablo Neruda / [in black, white, and orange: publisher's emblem] / [in black:] Selected Poems / A bi-lingual edition, edited by Nathaniel Tarn. Back: [in black:] Penguin Poets / Cover photo Diego Goldberg, Camera Press / For copyright reasons this edition is not for sale in the U.S.A. / [in black, white, and orange: publisher's emblem] / [in black, on left:] United Kingdom 75p / Australia $2.55 (recommended) / New Zealand $2.55 / Canada $3.25 / [on right:] Poetry / ISBN 0 14 / 042.185 8. Spine: [in black:] Pablo Neruda [slash] Selected Poems / ISBN 0 14 / 042. 185 8 / [in black, white, and orange: publisher's emblem].

Publication: Published in 1975 by Penguin Books, at 75p, as a volume in "The Penguin Poets" series. Printed by Hazell Watson & Viney Ltd., Aylesbury, Bucks.

Contents: According to Tarn's note, "This present selection represents a reduced model of the *Selected Poems* of Pablo Neruda, published by Jonathan Cape, London, in 1970 . . . This, in turn, had been based on a list provided by Pablo Neruda in July 1965 at the P.E.N. Conference in Bled, Yugoslavia . . . I have tried here to keep roughly the same balance in the coverage of individual volumes and in contributions by the four translators as prevailed in the earlier work." [May, 1972].

B8   Concorde   1975

Postcard. 6 1/8" × 4". Octavio Paz's "Concorde" in Spanish, with Tarn's English translation below, upside down, in black on stiff blue cover stock. Published as a "MenCard" by The Menard Press, London, in 1975, at 25p.

B9   He Who Hunted Birds in His Father's Village   1979

(a) *First edition:*

Title: GARY SNYDER / [rule] / He Who Hunted Birds / in His Father's Village / [rule] / THE DIMENSIONS OF A HAIDA MYTH / *With a Preface by Nathaniel Tarn* / [rule] / GREY FOX PRESS / Bolinas [device] California

Pagination: pp. [i–xiii] xi–xi [xii] xiii–xix [xx] 1–127 [128] 129–133 [134–140]; 8 ¾" × 5 5/8"; printed on wove paper.

Collation: pp. [i–ii] blank, [iii] half-title, [iv] photograph, [v] title, [vi] copyright, [vii] contents, [viii] blank, xi–xi text, [xii] blank, xiii–xix text, [xx] blank, 1–127 text, [128] blank, 129–133 text, [134] blank, [135] text, [136–140] blank.

Binding: Bound in brown cloth covered boards. Spine: [gold-stamped:] Gary Snyder *He Who Hunted Birds in His Father's Village* Grey Fox. White endpapers.

Dust jacket: Issued without dust jacket.

Publication: Published by Grey Fox Press in 1979 at $10.00.

Top: Tarn (left) with Octavio Paz, Cambridge, Mass., 1975. Bottom: Santiago Atitlán, 1979. From left: Nicolas Chiviliu (Ajkun *and* Principal Pasado), *Martin Prechtel* (Primer Mayor), *and Tarn.*

Contents: xiii–xix "By Way of a Preface," by Nathaniel Tarn. [From Tarn's "From Anthropologist to Informant," 1971].

(b) *First paper edition:*

As B9(a), save issued in stiff white wrappers. Front: [in black:] GARY SNYDER / [rule] / [in green:] He Who Hunted Birds / in His Father's Village / [in black:] [rule] / THE DIMENSIONS OF A HAIDA MYTH / [in black and green: illustration]; back: [photograph] / [in black:] GARY SNYDER [rule] / $5.00 0-912516-38-0; spine: [in black:] Gary Snyder *He Who Hunted Birds in His Father's Village* Grey Fox. Published at $5.00.

B10   **Time and the Highland Maya**   1982

Title: [running across recto and verso, in black:] *Barbara Tedlock* / [in grey: rule] / [in black:] TIME and the HIGHLAND MAYA / [in grey: decorative rules] / [in black:] *Albuquerque* / *UNIVERSITY of NEW MEXICO PRESS* / [in grey: decorative rule]

Pagination: pp. [i–iv] v–vii [viii] ix–xii [xiii–xiv] 1–10 [11–12] 13 [14–15] 16–17 [18–19] 20–22 [23–24] 25 [26] 27–28 [29–30] 31 [32] 33–38 [39] 40–44 [45–46] 47–54 [55] 56–62 [63] 64–66 [67–68] 69 [70] 71 [72–73] 74 [75] 76–77 [78–79] 80–82 [83] 84–85 [86–88] 89 [90] 91–100 [101–103] 104 [105–106] 107–131 [132] 133–140 [141] 142–150 [151–152] 153–160 [161] 162–163 [164–166] 167 [168–169] 170–171 [172] 173–178 [179–180] 181–187 [188] 189–211 [212] 213–225 [226] 227–239 [240] 241–245 [246–250]; 9 ½" × 6 3/8"; printed on wove paper.

Collation: pp. [i] half-title, [ii–iii] title, [iv] copyright, v–vii contents, [viii] half, ix–xii text, [xiii] half-title, [xiv] half-title, 1–10 text, [11] illustration, [12] half-title, 13 text, [14–15] illustrations, 16–17 text, [18–19] illustrations, 20–22 text, [23–24] illustrations, 25 text, [26] illustration, 27–28 text, [29–30] illustrations, 31 text , [32] illustration, 33–38 text, [39] illustration, 40–44 text, [45] illustration, [46] half-title, 47–54 text, [55] illustration, 56–59 [60] 61–62 text, [63] illustration, 64–66 text, [67–68] illustrations, 69 text, [70] illustration, 71 text, [72–73] illustrations, 74 text, [75] illustration, 76–77 text, [78–79] illustrations, 80–82 text, [83] illustration, 84–85 text, [86–87] illustrations, [88] half-title, 89 text, [90] illustration, 91–100 text, [101] illustration, text, [102] illustration, [103]–104 text, [105] illustration, [106] half-title, 107–131 text, [132] half-title, 133–140 text, [141] illustration, 142–150 text, [151] illustration, [152] half-title, 153–160 text, [161] illustration, 162–163 text, [164–166] illustrations, text, 167 text, [168] illustration, text, [169] illustration, 170–171 text, [172] illustration, 173–178 text, [179] illustration, [180] half-title, 181–

187 text, [188] half-title, 189–211 text, [212] half-title, 213–225 text, [226] half-title, 227–239 text, [240]–245 text, [246–250] blank.

Binding: Bound in black cloth-covered boards. Spine: [gold-stamped:] *Tedlock* TIME and the HIGHLAND MAYA / New / Mexico. Red endpapers.

Dust jacket: Issued in black dust jacket, white text. Front: TIME and the / HIGHLAND MAYA / [color photograph] / *Barbara Tedlock;* back: [listing of U.N.M. Press books]; spine: *Tedlock* / TIME and the HIGHLAND MAYA / New / Mexico. Flyleaves: front: [white, text in black:] TIME and the / HIGHLAND MAYA / *Barbara Tedlock* / *Foreword by Nathaniel Tarn* / [synopsis]; back: [synopsis continued, with extended quotation from Tarn's foreword] / [biographical note] / [publisher's emblem].

Publication: Published in June, 1981, by the University of New Mexico Press at $27.50.

Contents: xi "Foreword" [by Nathaniel Tarn].

C. Contributions to Periodicals

1957

C1   *Essay:* "Le Poète portugais Alberto de Lacerda," *Critique* (Paris), 117 (Feb., 1957), 113–23.

1958

C2   *Review:* "Sociologie: A Venture into the New Africa," *Critique* (Paris), 129 (Feb., 1958), 189–91.

1960

C3   *Poem:* "I Have No Ireland," *A Review of English Literature,* I, 4 (Oct., 1960), 19.

1961

C4   *Poem:* "On Reading Song vi, from Arthur Waley's 'Nine Songs,'" *Outposts,* 49, 7 (summer, 1961), 7.

1962

C5   *Poem:* "René Grousset Weeping," *Poetry and Audience,* 9 (March 9, 1962), 1.

C6   *Letter:* "Regina v. Penguin," *Encounter,* XVIII, 5 (May, 1962), 93.

C7   *Poem:* "Remembering Benares," *X,* 2, 3 (July, 1962), 235.

C8   *Poem:* "In the Greenhouse," *The Poetry Review,* LIII, 3 (summer, 1962), 182.

C9   *Poem:* "Out of Sleep, Beyonded," *Poetry and Audience,* 9 (Oct. 5, 1962), 7.

C10   *Poems:* "Adam Pacific," "Ranger Spacecraft," *Stand,* 6, 3 (1962), 6–7.

C11   *Poem:* "The Life We Do Not Lead," *Peacock,* 1 (1962), 12–3.

C12   *Poems:* "A Twilight for the Raj," "Some Peace from an Autumn Garden," *Endor,* 3 (1962), 16–7.

C13   *Poems:* "The Cure," "Fountains Abbey Under Snow," *Stand,* 7, 1 (1962), 52–3.

1963

C14   *Poem:* "Arashiyama," *Poetry and Audience,* 9 (May, 1963), 7.

C15   *Poems:* "Simeon Bar Yochai," "Abulafia," "The Master of the Name," "The Annunciation," "The Delivery," *The Listener* LXX, 1795 (Aug. 22, 1963), 267–68.

C16   *Poem:* "Red Sea Passage," *Outposts,* 58 (autumn, 1963), 5. [note: contents list "Nicholas Tarn"].

C17   *Poem:* "Burial, San Pedro Chenalho," *The Poetry Review,* LIV, 3 (autumn, 1963), 216.

C18   *Essay:* "L'Angleterre s'interroge," *Les Lettres Nouvelles* (Paris), 39 (Oct., 1963), 191–98.

C19   *Poems:* "Ely Cathedral," "The Moon in No," "To the Stillness of," "Last of the Chiefs," *The Poetry Review,* LIV, 1 (winter, 1963), 21–4.

C20   *Poems:* "The Wedding," "The Eden Foxes," "For the Death of Anton Weber, Particularly," *Ambit,* 15 (1963), 11–3.

C21   *Poems:* "Blackfly Melting," "Bring a Child Flowers," "The Omen," *Ambit,* 18 (1963/4), 14–6.

C22   *Poem:* "Prayer for Roses Newly Planted," *Agenda,* III, 3 (Dec./Jan., 1963/4), 15.

C23   *Essay:* "Le 'Cri du coeur' d'Ewart Milne," *Les Lettres Nouvelles* (Paris), 41 (Dec./Jan., 1963/64), 15–22.

1964

C24   *Poem:* "The Omen," *Developmental Medicine and Child Neurology,* VI, 1 (Feb., 1964), 87.

C25   *Interview:* "Nathaniel Tarn: Poetry and the Cabala," *The Jewish Chronicle* (March 13, 1964), 45.

C26   *Essay:* "Anatomie de la 'Pop culture,'" *Les Lettres Nouvelles* (Paris), 43 (April/May, 1964), 148–54.

C27   *Letter:* "Poetry Helplessly," *New Society,* 71 (June 2, 1964), 32.

C28   *Poem:* "Portrait of a Modern Jew," *Tribune,* 28, 22 (June 5, 1964), 11.

C29   *Poem:* "Master Spy," *Tribune,* 28, 28 (July 10, 1964), 12.

C30   *Poem:* "The Fineries," *Observer* (July 19, 1964), 23.

C31   *Poem:* "Old Savage/Young City," *Transatlantic Review,* 16 (summer, 1964), 67–72.

C32   *Poem:* "Virgo Speculatrix," *Granta,* 69 (Oct. 17, 1964), 11.

C33   *Poem:* "The Rights of Man," *Times Literary Supplement,* 3, 270 (Oct. 29, 1964), 981.

C34   *Review:* "Enlarging Our Horizons," *Tribune,* 28, 47 (Nov. 20, 1964), 14.

C35   *Review:* "Berliner Festwochen," *Le Journal des Poètes* (Brussels) (Dec., 1964), 5.

1965

C36   *Poem:* "The Floating Life," *Spectator,* 7127 (Jan., 1965), 143.

C37   *Review:* "Ida Kar in Cuba," *Tribune,* 29, 7 (Feb. 12, 1965), 15.

C38   *Poems:* "Head with Helmet," "Master Spy," "Persephone's Down," *Chelsea,* 16 (March, 1965), 98–100.

C39   *Poem:* "Das Leben das wir nicht fuhren," *Akzente* (Munich), 2 (April, 1965), 155–56.

C40   *Poem:* "The Stain," *Agenda,* 4, 1 (April/May, 1965), 27.

C41   *Poem:* "Last of the Chiefs," *Poésie Vivante* (Geneva), 11 (April/May, 1965), 4–5.

C42   *Poem:* "Dispersal," *Spectator,* 7141 (July 5, 1965), 604.

C43   *Poem:* "Dispersal," *Le Journal des Poètes* (Brussels), 7 (Sept., 1965), 3.

C44   *Poem:* "Eagle at Bookfair," *Outposts,* 65 (summer, 1965), 9.

C45   *Review:* "Companion for Bohemia," *Tribune,* 29, 33 (Aug. 13, 1965), 11.

C46   *Poem:* "Projections for an Eagle," *Quest,* I (Sept., 1965), 32–4.

C47   *Poem:* "The Eagles of Rome," *Granta,* 71 (Oct., 1965), 25.

C48   *Poems:* "Baptizing Masai," "Leaving a Grandmother," "Where Babylon Ends," *Ambit,* 25 (1965), 34–6.

C49   *Poem:* "Last of the Chiefs," *U.N. Special* (Dec., 1965), 23.

C50   *Essay:* "Poetry and Communication," *Vindrosen* (Copenhagen), 12, 1 (1965), 71–79.

C51   *Poem:* "Grief Is So Much a Now," *Adam,* 300 (1965), 195.

1966

C52   *Poems:* "The Wedding," "The Cure," *Jewish Quarterly,* 14, 2 (1966), 23.

C53   *Poem:* "The Satellite," *The Gownsman of St. David's College, Lampeter,* 12, 4 (Feb. 4, 1966), 3.

C54   *Poem:* "To the Stillness of," *Second City* (1966), 38.

C55   *Poems:* "Three Poems," *Plamen* (Prague) (April, 1966), 92–4.

C56   *Essay:* "Poésie et Communication," *Courrier du Centre International d'Etudes Poétiques* (Paris), 56 (Aug., 1966), 7–18.

C57   *Poem:* "After the Roaring Forties," *Spectator,* 7222 (Nov. 25, 1966), 690.

C58   *Poems:* "Three Poems," Hvedekorn (Copenhagen), 5 (1966), 147–49.

C59   *Poem:* "The King Returns," *Ambit,* 30 (1966/67), 30–3.

1967

C60   *Essay:* "Non un passé mais un avenir," *Nouvelle Revue Française* (Paris), XV, 172 (April 1, 1967), 946–52.

C61   *Essay:* "Pansies for Thought: Reflections on the Work of Claude Lévi-Strauss," *The Listener* (May 11, 1967) 618–19, 635.

C62   *Review:* "The Tantric Tradition," *The Listener* (June 22, 1967), 828.

C63   *Essay:* "These New Cape Editions," *The Bookseller* (July 29, 1967), 1138–40.

C64   *Poem:* "For Mahler," *Flourish* (spring, 1967), 2.

C65   *Poem:* "Your House," *The Scotsman* (Dec. 23, 1967), np.

C66   *Poems:* "Three Poems," *Siècle à mains,* 9 (1967), 43–6.

C67   *Poems:* "Park, Tulips, Wolves," "Your Age," *Haravec* (Lima), 3 (1967), 71–2.

1968

C68   *Poem:* "The Laurel Tree," *Agenda,* 6, 2 (spring, 1968), 31–3.

C69   *Review:* "Thirty Thousand Years of Art," *The Times* (Sept. 14, 1968), 20.

C70   *Review:* "Elegant for Whom?" *The Times* (Oct. 12, 1968), 25.

C71   *Interview:* "Discussion," *Etudes littéraires* (Montreal), I, 3 (Dec., 1968), 379–80.

C72   *Review:* "The Once and Future King," *The Times* (Dec. 14, 1968), 20.

C73   *Review:* "Art in an African Society," *The Times* (Dec. 21, 1968), 18.

C74   *Essay:* "Notes sur le thème de la diffusion de la poésie en territoire Anglo-Saxon," *Le Journal des Poètes* (Brussels), 7 (1968), 6–7.

C75   *Poems:* "Two Poems from Wales," *Haravec* (Lima), 5 (1968), 51–2.

C76   *Poem:* "The Laurel Tree," *El Corno Emplumado* (Mexico City), 26 (1968), 30–1.

1969

C77   *Review:* "The Marching Columns," *The Times Saturday Review* (Jan. 25, 1969), 22.

C78   *Review:* "A Key to Human Communication," *The Times Saturday Review* (Feb. 22, 1969), 22.

C79   *Review:* "The Square Root of Hip," *London Magazine,* 8, 11 (Feb., 1969), 85–90.

C80   *Review:* "Under the Volcano," *The Times Saturday Review* (May 17, 1969), 20.

C81   *Poem:* "October: The Field of Merit," *Forum* (summer, 1969), 5.

C82   *Poem:* "October: The Dark Night," *Peace News*, 1737 (Oct. 10, 1969), 6.

C83   *Poems:* "Concert," "On Seeing a Wheatear for the First Time," *New Measure,* 10 (1969), 61–2.

C84   *Poems:* "Giovanni di Paolo on Parade in New York City," "Elizavine of Elliotte at Cantorberry or the X-Ray of Thursday," "You Are Becoming Near to Me," *Micromegas,* III, 1 (1969), 16–8.

C85   *Poem:* "El Laurel," *Union* (Havana), 3 (1969), 24–8.

1970

C86   *Poem:* "The Great Odor of Summer," *WAR!,* 1 (May 11, 1970), 5-8.

C87   *Poem:* "El Gran Olor del Verano," *Siempre Suplemento Cultural* (Mexico City) (May, 1970), xvi.

C88   *Poem:* Paolo in Thule," *Resurgence,* 3, 1 (May/June, 1970), 11.

C89   *Poem:* "Fragments from the Prayers Made on Behalf of Nathaniel Tarn,"*Alcheringa,* 1 (fall, 1970), 58-62.

C90   *Poems:* "A Nowhere for Vallejo: sections II, V, VII, XI," *Sumac,* 2, IV (fall, 1970), 40-7.

C91   *Poem:* "The Great Odor of Summer,"*Journal Rhizone* (Nov., 1970), 4-5.

C92   *Poem:* "The Female Aspect of God," *Tree,* 1 (winter, 1970), 54-5.

C93   *Poems:* "From 'A Nowhere for Vallejo,'" "Valedictions," *Raster* (Amsterdam), IV, 3 (1970), 257-64.

C94   *Poems:* "The Beaches," "Accidents," "Valedictions," *Anonym,* 5/6 (1970), 12-4.

C95   *Poems:* "For Buffy Sainte-Marie," "Choices," "Accidents," *Raster* (Amsterdam), IV, 4 (winter, 1970/71), 424-29.

1971

C96   *Poems:* "For Buffy Sainte-Marie," "The Great Odor of Summer," *Chicago Review,* 22, 3/4 (spring, 1971), 5-12.

C97   *Poem:* "From 'A Nowhere for Vallejo,'" *Antaeus,* 2 (spring, 1971), 86- 92.

C98   *Poem:* "To Meltzer at Bolinas," *Tree,* 2 (summer, 1971), 24-9.

C99   *Poem:* "She Flies the Islands," *All You Can Eat* (June 24, 1971), 15.

C100   *Essay:* "A Latin Walt Whitman," *The New York Times* (Oct. 22, 1971), 34.

C101 *Poem:* "Amor Americano," *The Desert Rose* (fall, 1971), 2.

C102 *Essay:* "The Last Word: A Nobel for Neruda," *The New York Times Book Review* (Nov. 7, 1971), 55.

C103 *Poems:* "Swimmer," "Aging Hands," "Scorpions," "A Nowhere for Vallejo," *Chicago Review,* 22, 2/3 (winter, 1971), 143–52.

C104 *Review:* "Willie Masters' Lonesome Wife," *The New York Times Book Review* (Nov. 14, 1971), 5.

C105 *Review:* "Art Far from Us," *The New York Times Book Review* (Dec. 12, 1971), 7, 37.

C106 *Poem:* "From 'Portraits': Anton Bruckner," *The,* 8 (1971), 10–1.

C107 *Poems:* "The First Persephone," "The Third Persephone," "The Tenth Persephone," "The Kitchen," *Raster* (Amsterdam), V, 3 (1971), 406–14.

1972

C108 *Poem:* "From 'Lyrics for the Bride of God': Seen as a Bird," *Clear Creek,* II, 2 (March, 1972), 56–7.

C109 *Poem:* "From 'Lyrics for the Bride of God': Section: The Artemision," *Fervent Valley,* 2 (summer, 1972), [34–5].

C110 *Poems:* "The First Persephone," "The Second Persephone," "The Seventh Persephone," "The Ninth Persephone," *Poetry Review,* 63 (autumn, 1972), 236–41.

C111 *Poem:* "From 'Lyrics for the Bride of God': Section: The Artemision," *Unmuzzled Ox,* 1, 4 (autumn, 1972), [38–41].

C112 *Poem:* "From 'Portraits': René Margritte," *Toothpick, Lisbon & The Orca Islands,* 2, 1/2 (fall, 1972), 33–4.

C113 *Essay:* "From Anthropologist to Informant: A Field Record of Gary Snyder," *Alcheringa,* 4 (autumn, 1972), 104–113.

C114 *Poem:* "Olvido Inolvidable," *Books Abroad,* 46, 4 (autumn, 1972), 609.

C115 *Poem:* "From 'Lyrics for the Bride of God': Section: The Artemision," *Seizure Magazine,* 1, 2 (fall/winter, 1972), 61–2.

C116 *Poem:* "From 'Lyrics for the Bride of God,'" *Tree,* 3 (winter, 1972), 14–20.

C117 *Poem:* "From 'Lyrics for the Bride of God': The Jubilation," *Chicago Review,* 23, 3 (winter, 1972), 7–9.

C118 *Essay/Poems:* "Towards Any Geography/Towards Any America Whatsoever," "America," "From the Point of View of Anchises," "She Becomes Our Lady," "She Tears Him Apart and Sells Him Piecemeal," "She Turns Black," "She Is a Child," *IO,* 2 (1972), 6–10, 240–53.

C119 *Poems:* "The Walls of Santiago," "The Roses of Guatemala," *Stooge,* 7 (1972), [28–30].

C120 *Poems:* "Tres Desde Pachichiyut," "For Those in Washington," *Stooge,* 6 (1972), [10–31].

C121 *Poems:* "Airline for Ariadne," "First Cardinal," "Thinking Her Name," *Ambit,* 51 (1972), 17–20.

C122 *Poems:* "From 'Lyrics for the Bride of God': The Inner Seduction," "The Persephones," *Salamander,* 1 (1972), 1–3, 61–79.

C123 *Poem:* "From 'Lyrics for the Bride of God': Section: The Artemision," *Raster* (Amsterdam), VI, 4 (winter, 1972/73), 564–76.

1973

C124 *Poem:* "From 'Lyrics for the Bride of God': Section: The Invisible Bride," *Fuse,* 3 (March, 1973), 16–18.

C125 *Poem:* "From 'Lyrics for the Bride of God': Section: The Invisible Bride," *Truck,* 11 (spring, 1973), 17–19.

C126 *Poems:* "From 'Lyrics for the Bride of God': The Kitchen (4–6), *Red Crow,* 2 (Spring, 1973), 198–203.

C127 *Poems:* "The Creature," "Provincial Morning," "To Certain, Mainly Younger, Women," *The Painted Bird Quarterly,* 1, 1 (fall, 1973), 10–13.

C128 *Review:* "Tajos," *The New York Times Book Review* (Nov. 18, 1973), 45.

1974

C129   *Poems:* "Fossil Song," "The Microcosm," "The Aura," *The Painted Bird Quarterly,* 1, 2 (spring, 1974), 32–4.

C130   *Letter:* "On Neruda," *American Poetry Review* (May/June, 1974), 70.

C131   *Poem:* "From 'Lyrics for the Bride of God': Section: The Seduction," *Tree,* 4 (winter, 1974), 75–80.

C132   *Poem:* "Earth-Till," *Ironwood,* 4 (Dec., 1974), 42.

1975

C133   *Poems:* "The Gate of Esperaunce," "The Indecision," *Sailing the Road Clear,* III (Feb., 1975), 13–14.

C134   *Poem:* "Poem 5, from 'The Fire Poem,'" *L'Europa Letteraria E Artistica,* 4/5 (May/June, 1975), 66–7.

C135   *Poems:* "Standing Rock Sequence, The Dakotas," "Earth-Till," "The Northern Lover," "The Scribner's Room, Princeton Library," *Northwest Review,* XV, 1 (summer, 1975), 52–9.

C136   *Poems:* "The Satellite," "Ranger Spacecraft," *Listening and Writing,* (autumn, 1975), 5–6.

C137   *Poem:* "From 'Lyrics for the Bride of God': Section: La Traviata," *Tri-Quarterly,* 34 (fall, 1975), 158–78.

C138   *Poem:* "From 'The Fire Poem': Poem 5," *Beloit Poetry Journal,* 26, 1 (fall, 1975), 63.

C139   *Essay/Poems/Interview:* "From 'Atlantis: An Auto-Anthropology,'" "Three Comings to the House of Leaves," "Narrative of the Readings in Chicago," "An Interview with Nathaniel Tarn" [by Jed Rasula and Mike Erwin], *Boundary 2,* IV, 1 (fall, 1975), 1–55.

C140   *Poem:* "The Invisible Bride," *Los,* I (1975), 23–7.

C141   *Poem:* "Food," *Famous* (1975), [35–6].

C142   *Poem:* "From 'Lyrics for the Bride of God,'" *Sixpack,* 9 (1975), 174–80.

1976

C143   *Poem:* "The College," *Via,* 1 (May, 1976), 42–7.

C144   *Essay:* "Alaskan Artists of the World Reunite," *Survival International Review,* I, 14 (spring, 1976), 34.

C145   *Poem:* "From 'Lyrics for the Bride of God': Section: The Invisible Bride," *Shocks,* 6 (1976), 91–4.

C146   *Essay:* "The Heraldic Vision: Some Cognitive Models for Ethnopoetics," *Alcheringa* (New Series) 2, 2 (1976), 23–41.

1977

C147   *Poem:* "From 'Alashka': Pendant to the Ground" (with Janet Rodney), *Credences,* 4 (March, 1977), 21–9.

C148   *Poem:* "Narrative of the Heartbeat" (with Janet Rodney), *New World Journal,* I, 2/3 (spring, 1977), 56–9.

C149   *Poem:* "Willow," *Hand Book,* 1 (winter, 1977), 59–62.

C150   *Review:* "Landscape Papers," *American Book Review,* 1, 1 (Dec., 1977), 7.

C151   *Poem:* "Narrative of the Spiders," *Poetry Review,* 66, 3/4 (1977), 175–77.

C152   *Poem:* "Narrative of the Great Animal" (with Janet Rodney), *New Directions,* 34 (1977), 69–73.

C153   *Poems:* "Three Poems from 'Alashka'" (with Janet Rodney), *New Wilderness Letter* (Poetry Supplement), 1, 3 (Dec., 1977/Jan., 1978), [3].

1978

C154   *Note:* "Cultural Ripoff," *Raven's Bones* (Feb., 1978), 4.

C155   *Poem:* "[From: 'Alashka': Cities]" (with Janet Rodney), *Bezoar,* 12 (June, 1978), 5–9.

C156   *Poems:* "The Oldest Guide," "Black Mountain," *Plucked Chicken,* 3 (June, 1978), 67-8.

C157   *Poems:* "Three Proses," *Tamarisk,* II, 1 (winter, 1978), 31.

C158   *Poem:* "From 'Alashka'" (with Janet Rodney), *Hand Book,* 2 (1978), 57-64.

C159   *Poems:* "JR/NT: Each to the Other," "Narrative/Invocation of, and to, the Place Klukwan," *Paper Air,* 1, 3 (1978), [1], 29-32.

1979

C160   *Poem:* "Narrative of the Spiders," *Schuim* (Antwerp), 1/2 (Feb., 1979), 44-51.

C161   *Poems:* "Four Poems from 'North Rim,'" *The Atlantic Review* (spring, 1979), 46-7.

C162   *Poem/Essay:* "Journal of the Laguna de San Ignacio," "Open Letter Regarding a Proposal for an Order of Silence," *Montemora,* 5 (1979), 74-80, 176-83.

C163   *Notes:* "Archeology," "Newfoundland," "Of," "Sparrow," *Unmuzzled Ox [The Poet's Encyclopedia],* IV, IV/V (1979), 19, 195, 197, 254.

C164   *Poem:* "For Toby Olson," *Hand Book,* 3 (1979), 12.

C165   *Poem:* "Desde Pachichiyut," *Gaceta del Fonda de Cultura Economica* (Mexico City) (1979), 106.

C166   *Poems:* "Between Delaware and Hudson: 5 & 8," "Narrative of the Great Animal," "From 'The Ground of Our Great Admiration for Nature'" (with Janet Rodney), *Po&Sie* (Paris), 8 (1979), 43-53.

1980

C167   *Poem:* "From 'The Journal of Laguna de San Ignacio,'" *Credences,* 3, 3/4 (March, 1980), 83-90.

C168 *Poem:* "Letter from Homer" (with Janet Rodney), *Sun & Moon,* 9/10 (summer, 1980), 28–30.

C169 *Poem:* "Willow," *Po&Sie* (Paris), 12 (1980), 42–5.

C170 *Poem:* "Palenque," *Stonechat,* 1 (Nov., 1980), 24–8.

C171 *Poem:* "Palenque," *Montemora,* 7 (1980), 71–7. Note: drawings by NT on 70 & 96.

C172 *Poem:* "Flight from the Mountaintop," *Imprint,* 3 (1980), 37–40.

C173 *Poems:* "Eight from Hokkaido," *Zero,* V (1980), 44–51.

1981

C174 *Poems:* "From 'Weekend in Mexico,'" *Oasis,* 31 (1981), 43–6.

C175 *Essay:* "Metaphors of Relative Elevation, Position, and Ranking in Popol Vuh" (with Martin Prechtel), *Estudios De Cultura Maya* (Mexico City), XIII (1981), 105–23.

C176 *Essay:* "Archeology, Elegy, Architecture: A Poet's Program for Lyric," *Sub-Stance,* 28 (1981), 3–24.

1982

C177 *Poem:* "Thus Love," *The University City Press,* X, 2 (Jan., 1982), 24.

C178 *Poem:* "Narrative of the Flight from the Mountaintop," *Telegram,* 3 (1982), 19–23.

C179 *Poem:* "North Rim," *Conjunctions,* 2 (1982), 7–17.

C180 *Poems:* "Three Months in Which to Live," "Opening Out a Line of Mandelstam's," "Energetically Singing Against Voracious Earth," "And Even the Republic Must Have an End," "The Tree of Another World," *Sulfur,* 4 (1982), 133–7.

C181 *Poem:* "Flight from the Mountaintop," *Conjunctions,* 3 (1982), 114–18.

C182   *Poem:* "Eyes Alone with Their Shadows," *Perception/O.Ars,* 2 (1982), 11.

1983

C183   *Poem:* "Eyes Alone with Their Shadows," *2 Plus 2* (Lausaunne), 1 (autumn, 1983), 32.

C184   *Poems:* "An Immigrant's Address," "The Going of All the Dogs," *Correspondence* (Lausaunne), 2 (1983), 54–5.

C185   *Poem:* "The White Widow," *Sagetrieb,* 2, 3 (winter, 1983), 27–8.

C186   *Poems:* "For the Rules of Flight," "Or That the President Would Abdicate," "Rainer Werner Moves His Lady from Hollywood to Heaven," *Luna Tack,* IV, 7 (Dec., 1983), 7–11.

C187   *Poems:* "Persephone West," "Twin Star to Persephone West," "Eyes Watching Up-Sky," *Tarasque,* 1 (1983), 4–6.

C188   *Poem:* "Opening Out a Line of Mandelstam's," *Correspondence* (Lausaunne), 3 (1983), 9.

C189   *Poem:* "[The ritual . . ."], *Kosmos,* 7 (1983), 45.

C190   *Poem:* "Dog Viewing Deer," *Sulfur,* 8 (1983), 86–91.

C191   *Poems:* "Nor Was It Possible," "The June Flower," "'The Selection of Heaven,'" "His Eyes Looking Forward and Upward," "From the Mercer Museum's Windows," "Reaching for Hölderlin," "Cliffs of the Ultimate Record," "At a Meeting, the Cry," "Of a Marriage Made Within the Great Light," "Speaking with the Dead Along the Canal," "The Last Grand Rain," "Lying Beside Her," "Of a Marriage Returned to the Great Light," *Conjunctions,* 4 (1983), 155–67.

C192   *Poems:* "Entering Into This," "Animal Bride," "Peredur West," "Death Fear—Yet of Another," *Conjunctions,* 5 (1983), 228–34.

1984

C193   *Poem:* "The Bay Dies of Pollution & Decoys Rise in Price," *Exquisite Corpse,* 2, 1 (Jan./Feb., 1984), 9.

C194   *Essay:* "Americans in Paris," *Exquisite Corpse,* 2, 5/7 (May/June, 1984), 17.

C195   *Poems:* "Nine Poems from 'Seeing America First,'" *Credences* (New Series), 3, 1 (spring, 1984), 24–32.

C196   *Essay:* "Child As Father to Man in the American Universe," *American Poetry,* 1, 2 (winter, 1984), 67–85.

C197   *Essay:* "Dr. Jekyll, the Anthropologist Emerges and Marches into the Notebook of Mr. Hyde, the Poet," *Conjunctions,* 6 (1984), 266–80.

C198   *Essay:* "Fresh Frozen Fenix: Random Notes on the Sublime, the Beautiful, and the Ugly in the Postmodern Era," *New Literary History,* XVI (winter, 1984/85), 417–25.

1985

C199   *Essay/Poems:* "Newly Saying the Already Said: An Attached Comment in Honor of Keiji Nishitani," "In Memoriam: Kholiakov," "Hans Memling," "Metamorphosis of Spider with Crab," *H/Ear* (Melbourne), 8 (spring, 1985), 384–94.

C200   *Poem:* "Jonah's Saddle," *Tyuonyi,* 1 (1985), 35–42.

C201   *Poems:* "From the Book of Songs Provisionally Entitled at the Time of Writing 'All These Shitty Little Places in New Jersey,'" *Conjunctions,* 7 (1985), 210–23.

C202   *Interview:* "Reflector Interview: Nathaniel Tarn," *Reflector* (1985), 13–6.

1986

C203   *Poems:* "From 'Ethnographies,'" *Hambone,* 6 (fall, 1986), 57–64.

C204   *Essay:* "Neruda and Indigenous Culture," *Sulfur,* 15 (1986), 169–73.

C205   *Poems/Review:* "Remission Bardo," "Metamorphosis of Spider," "The Land in Question," *"Popol Vuh: The Definitive Edition,"* *Conjunctions,* 9 (1986), 121–27, 273–78.

C206   *Poem:* "Insofar As No Hope Is Left to Him," *People to People,* 1 (1986), 8.

C207   *Poems:* "Winter Oasis," "The Life-Sitter," *Osiris,* 22 (1986), 14–5.

C208   *Poem:* "Metamorphosis of Spider into Crab," *Ninth Decade,* 6 (1986), 40–2.

C209   *Poem:* "Prototractatus," *Tyuonyi,* 2 (1986), 158–9.

D. Translations by Nathaniel Tarn

D1 "Leviathan" [Pablo Neruda]. *The Penguin Book of Verse Translation,* George Steiner, ed. London: Penguin Books, 1966. 314–15.

D2 "Nine Poems from *Stèles* and *Thibet*" [Victor Segalen]. *MPT* (summer, 1966), 2:2–4.

D3 "From the Heights of Macchu Picchu "[Pablo Neruda]. *The Rotarian* (June, 1967), 110, 6:18–9.

D4 "Cemetary at Vilcashuaman" [Antonio Cisneros]. *Agenda* (autumn, 1968), 6, 3:103.

D5 "Nicodemus Speaking," [Cintio Vitier]. *Times Literary Supplement* (Nov. 14, 1968), 1291.

D6 "Six Poems from *Stèles*" [Victor Segalen]. *Unicorn Journal* (1969), 19:67–73.

D7 "Cuban Verse" [Cintio Vitier, E. Diego, José Lezama Lima, Guillermo Rivera, Belkis Cuza Malé]. *Isis* (Jan. 29, 1969), 12–3.

D8 "Verses" [Vladimir Holan]. *Tribune* (March 14, 1969), 11.

D9 "Summons of the Desirer," "An Obscure Meadow Lures Me" [José Lezama Lima]. *Mundus Artium* (winter, 1969), III, 1:46–9.

D10 "Nicodemus Speaking" [Cintio Vitier]. *Anthroposophical Quarterly* (spring, 1970), XV, 1:8.

D11 "De Las Furias y Las Penas" [Pablo Neruda]. *Door and Mirrors: Fiction and Poetry from Spanish America,* Hortense Carpenter and Janet Brof, eds. New York: Grossman, 1972. 124–7.

D12 "Rabinal-Achi: Part IV." *Alcheringa* (summer, 1971), 2:74–93.

D13 "From *Interludio Idílico:* Coda," "From *Cancionero Del Claro Palacio: The Radiant Palace,*" "*From Cancionero De Abajo: Song of the Rain,*" "From *Canciones Sin Su Musica* 1, 2, 11" [Tomas Segovia]. *Quarterly Review of Literature* (1972), XVIII, 1/2: 237–40.

D14 "Man" [Homero Aridjis]. *Boston University Journal* (spring, 1974), XXII, 2:31.

D15 "El tenia un planta azul," "El ser que yo amo me pega," "No se sentía bien," "Numeros," "Piedra sellada." *Blue Spaces: Selected Poems of Homero Aridjis,* Kenneth Rexroth, ed. New York: Seabury, 1974. 133–4, 143–4, 153–4, 159–60, 167–8, 169–70.

D16 "Selections" [Lezama Lima]. *The Borzoi Anthology of Latin American Literature.* E. Ramirez Monegal, ed. New York: Knopf, 1977.

D17 "Brevet" [Michel Deguy]. *Sub-Stance* (1979), 23/4:31–6.

D18 "Twenty Years Later" [Jacinto Cua Pospoy], with Martin Prechtel. *Sulfur* (1981), 1:21–7.

D19 "From: 'El Golpe Avisa'" [Hector Manjarrez]. *Sulfur* (1981), 2:59–64.

D20 "Seven Poems by Victor Segalen." *The Random House Book of Twentieth-Century French Poetry,* Paul Auster, ed. New York: Random House, 1982. 76–83.

D21 "Three Poems from *Gisants*" [Michel Deguy]. *Conjunctions* (1986), 9:24–6.

E. Contributions to Anthologies

E1   "Ely Cathedral," *The Pattern of Poetry,* William Kean Seymour and John Smith, eds. London: Burke, 1963. 48.

E2   "The Cure," "Fountains Abbey Under Snow," *Handbook of the Cheltenham Festival of Literature* (Sept. 30–Oct. 4, 1963). 48–9.

E3   "Baptising Masai," *New Poems 1965: A P.E.N. Anthology of Contemporary Poetry,* C.V. Wedgewood, ed. London: Hutchinson, 1966. 160.

E4   "Eagle Hunt," *Poems Addressed to Hugh MacDiarmid and Presented to Him on His Seventy-Fifth Birthday,* Duncan Glen, ed. Preston: Akros Publications, 1967. 58–9.

E5   "For Louis Brunel's Chambermaid from the Poets," *Christopher Perret Memorial Volume.* Geneva: Poésie Vivante, 1967. 206.

E6   "For the Death of Anton Webern Particularly," *Music & Sweet Poetry,* John Bishop, ed. London: John Baker, 1968. 39.

E7   "The Ministry of Death," *Explorations,* Murray Mindlin and Chaim Bermant, eds. Chicago: Quadrangle Books, 1968. 297–8.

E8   "The Satellite," "Ranger Spacecraft," "Head with Helmet," *Frontier of Going: An Anthology of Space Poetry,* John Fairfax, ed. London: Panther Books, 1969. 46, 76, 84.

E9   "The Life We Do Not Lead," "The Cure," "The Wedding," "The Rights of Man," *Poems from Poetry and Jazz in Concert,* Jeremy Robson, ed. London: Souvenir Press, 1969. 32–5.

E10   "The Work Laid Before Us," *Some of "It",* David Mairowitz, ed. London: Knullar Ltd., 1969. 92–5.

E11   "Last of the Chiefs," "Markings," "From 'The Poetry of Politics,'" *British Poetry Since 1945,* Edward Lucie-Smith, ed. Harmondsworth: Penguin Books, 1970. 248–50, 396–99.

E12   "Last of the Chiefs," "Projections for an Eagle," "From 'A Nowhere for Vallejo,'" "From 'The Beautiful Contradictions,'" *23 Modern British Poets,* John Matthias, ed. Chicago: The Swallow Press, 1971. 289–309.

E13   "Rabinal Achi: Act IV," *Shaking the Pumpkin: Traditional Poetry of the Indian North Americas,* Jerome Rothenberg, ed. Garden City: Doubleday, 1972. 236–59.

E14   "From 'Macchu Picchu,'" *Mirrors: An Introduction to Literature,* John R. Knott, Jr. and Christopher R. Reaske, eds. San Francisco: Canfield Press, 1972. 286–7.

E15   "For Buffy Saint-Marie," *Best Poems of 1971: Borestone Mountain Poetry Awards 1972.* Palo Alto: Pacific Books, 1972. 109–10.

E16   "The Microcosm," *A Keepsake from the New Library at the School of Oriental & African Studies.* London: University of London, 1973. [11].

E17   "From *The Beautiful Contradictions:* Sections 2 & 5." *Open Poetry,* Ronald Gross and George Quasha, eds. New York: Simon and Schuster, 1973. 214–16.

E18   "La Notte Oscura," *Almanacco Internazionale Dei Poeti 1973,* Giancarlo Vigorelli, ed. Milan: Giorgio Borletti Editore, 1973. 336–7.

E19   "Olvido Inolvidable," *The Perpetual Present: The Poetry and Prose of Octavio Paz,* Ivar Ivask, ed. Norman: University of Oklahoma Press, 1973. 130.

E20   "Da 'La Belle Contraddizioni," *Almanacco Internazionale Dei Poeti,* 1974. Milan: La Pergola Edizioni, 1974. 126–32.

E21   "From 'Lyrics for the Bride of God': The Dictation," *Active Anthology,* George Quasha, ed. Fremont, Michigan: Sumac Press, 1974. 175–79.

E22   "Bring a Child Flowers," *The Roses Race Around Her Name,* Jonathan Cott, ed. New York: Stonehill, 1974. 87.

E23   "From *The Beautiful Contradictions:* Section Five." *America: A Prophecy,* Jerome Rothenberg and George Quasha, eds. New York: Random House, 1974. 157–8.

E24   "Aging Hands," *A Book of Poems.* Np: Sophomore Literary Festival Council, 1975. 4–5.

E25   "The Kitchen (8): The Archeology of the Seduction," *The Doctor Generosity Poets,* Charles Shahoud Hanna, ed. Wescosville: Damascus Road Press, 1975. 210-11.

E26   "At Gloucester, Mass., After Foreign Travel," *For Neruda, For Chile,* Walter Lowenfels, ed. Boston: Beacon Press, 1975. 201-3.

E27   "Rene Grousset Weeping at the Doors of the Shosoin," *21 Years of Poetry and Audience,* Tom Wharton and Wayne Brown, eds. Breakish: Aquila Poetry, 1976. 38.

E28   "From 'Lyrics for the Bride of God': Section: The Artemision," *Intrepid Anthology,* Allen Deloach, ed. Buffalo: Intrepid Press, 1976. 333-7.

E29   "Narrative of the Great Animal" (with Janet Rodney), *New Directions, 34,* James Lauglin, ed. New York: New Directions, 1977. 69-73.

E30   "The Damaske Rose," *Madeira and Toasts for Basil Bunting's 75th Birthday,* Jonathan Williams, ed. North Carolina: Jargon Society, 1977. np.

E31   "Tactic" (with Janet Rodney), *Ecology and Consciousness,* Richard Grossinger, ed. Richmond: California: North Atlantic Books, 1978. 24.

E32   "From 'Lyrics for the Bride of God': The Kitchen, Sparagmos," *A Big Jewish Book,* Jerome Rothenberg, ed., with Harris Lenowitz and Charles Doria. Garden City: Anchor Press/Doubleday, 1978. 39-41, 565-8.

E33   "From *The Beautiful Contradictions,*" *Poeti Inglesi Del 900,* Robert Sansei, ed. Milan: Tascabili Bompiani, 1978. 510-27.

E34   "Where Babylon Ends," *Voices Within the Ark: Modern Jewish Poets,* Howard Schwartz and Anthony Rudolf, eds. New York: Avon Books, 1980. 664-5.

E35   "From 'Records of the Posthumous Life,'" *For Rexroth,* Geoffrey Gardner, ed. New York: The Ark, 1980, 376-8.

E36   "The Beautiful Contradictions," "The Silence," "The Third Person," "The Persephones," "A Preface," "The Jubilation," "At Gloucester," (English and French texts), *Vingt Poètes Américans,* Jacques Roubaud, ed. Paris: Gallimard, 1980. 239-85.

E37 "Selectie uit de gedichten van Nathaniel Tarn," *Levenstenkens &*
Doodssinjalen, H.C. Berge, ed. Amsterdam: Uitgeverid De Bezige Bij, 1980.
156–77.

E38 "Robert Redfield," *Totems and Teachers: Perspectives on the History of*
Anthropology, Sydel Silverman, ed. New York: Columbia University Press,
1981. 255–84.

E39 "Fragments from the Prayers Made on Behalf of Nathaniel Tarn,"
Symposium of the Whole, Jerome Rothenberg and Diane Rothenberg, eds.
Berkeley: University of California Press, 1983. 408–13.

E40 "Metaphors of Relative Evaluation, Position, and Ranking in
Popol Vuh" (with Martin Prechtel), *Nuevas Perspectivas Sobre El Popol Vuh,*
Robert M. McCarmack and Francis Morales Santos, eds. Guatemala City:
Editorial Piedra Santa, 1983. 163–79.

E41 "Desde Pachichiyut," *Cuaderno de Traducciones.* Mexico City: Fondo
de Cultura Económica, 1984. 116–17.

E42 "From *The Beautiful Contradictions,*" *Reflections: The Anthropological*
Muse, J. Iain Prattis, ed. Washington, D.C.: American Anthropological
Association, 1985. 120–28.

E43 "From *The Beautiful Contradictions,*" *Permutations: Readings in Science*
and Literature, Joan Digby and Bob Brier, eds. New York: Quill, 1985. 282–
83.

Appendix 1. Heteronyms

According to Nathaniel Tarn, "The poet's very first privilege of selecting the name under which his work will make its way in the world has always been a commonplace among Europeans. All the more so when names have been dubious or uncertain for any one of many possible reasons. Such was often the case for immigrants from Central and Eastern Europe whose names, presented at the Customs and Immigration Services, could not fit comfortably within the reaches of English or American tongues. The name Nathaniel Tarn happened to be born with was such a customs name and bore no relation to the original name."

The bulk of Nathaniel Tarn's work has appeared under that name, though early on he published a number of ephemeral pieces under the "heteronym" Michel Tavriger in *Parisian Weekly Information*, a tourist journal, as well as a book. Further, most of his anthropological work has appeared under the name of E. Michael Mendelson. Following is a checklist of that material.

I. Michel Tavriger

Book

AP1   La Légende de Saint-Germain-des-Prés   1950

Title: La / légende / de / Saint-Germain-des-Prés / [publisher's emblem] / LA ROULOTTE / 25, RUE BONAPARTE, Vie / PARIS

Collation: pp. [1–72]; 9 ¼ " × 6 3/8"; printed on glossy wove paper.

Pagination: pp. [1] half-title, [2] copyright, [3] title, [4–21] text, [22–69] photographs with captions, [70] blank, [71] colophon, [72] blank.

Binding: Bound in cream paper over boards. Front: LA LEGENDE DE / SAINT-GERMAIN-DES-PRES / [publisher's emblem] / LA ROULOTTE; spine: LEGENDE. Photographically decorated endpapers.

Dust jacket: Issued in dust jacket with black and white photograph of a woman on front and back. Front: [in red] la / légende / de / St Germain / des Prés / [in white:] The Legend of / St Germain-des-Prés; back: [in white, lower left:] Anouk Aymée. fugitire prin- / cesse de Saint-Germain- / des-Prés ... hier encore à l'écran / Juliette de Vérone. / [lower right:] Juliet of Verona on the / screen. of Saint-Germain-des- / Prés in real life. Anouk Aymée / is a legendary princess ...; spine: [red and white bars, in black:] LEGENDE; [front and rear flyleaves, at foot:] [publisher's emblem] / LA ROULOTTE / [device] / PARIS.

Publication: Published by La Roulotte, Paris, September 10, 1950, in an edition of fifty numbered copies. Photographs by Serge Jacques, design by Marcel Jacno, preface by Pierre Seghers.

Contents: pp. [5] "Between" [Seghers' preface, trans. by M.T.], [6–21] "La légende de Saint Germain-des-Prés" by M.T. [French and English facing texts].

Note: "I was fascinated with the whole legend of St. Germain — not just with Sartre and Co., but also with everything that grew out of it — so I suggested to friends that we do a picture book about it. I wrote the text as Michel Tavriger, Serge Jacques took the photographs, and Marcel Jacno designed the book. The publisher saw it as a potential tourist item, and thought my text wasn't popular enough. So either he or one of his minions rewrote my text. I think he kept my basic ideas, but still I don't consider it to be mine anymore. Incidentally, the book was the major cause of my expulsion from the Surrealists. One of the young heir apparents of André Breton brought to Breton's attention the fact that Tavriger had committed the crime of being interested in the existentialists, all of whom were anathema to the movement. This was brought up in full council and I was disciplined. I stood up and said I wouldn't stand for such a thing and marched out of the meeting, along with two friends and my girlfriend. Breton lost four people on that one row, though things like that were happening every week with the Surrealists. It is the French brand of literary terrorism."

Articles (in *Parisian Weekly Information, Cette Semaine à Paris,* unless otherwise indicated):

AP2   "Paris Roundabout:Miro at Maeght; La Rose Rouge," "Night Clubs: At La Camargo," Nov. 24, 1948.

AP3   "Paris Roundabout: Picasso Pottery," "Night Clubs: The Puerta Del Sol," "Cabarets: A La Villa D'Este, La Puerta Del Sol," "Fred Adison," Dec. 8, 1948.

AP4   "Paris Preview," Dec. 15, 1948.

AP5   "Paris Roundabout," "Cabarets: Le Drap D'or," Dec. 22, 1948.

AP6   "Peace on Earth to Men of Good Will . . . ," Dec. 29, 1948.

AP7   "Night Clubs: At the Carroll's," "Cabarets: Au Carroll's," Jan. 12, 1949.

AP8   "Paris Roundabout: Victor Brauner and Hans Hoffman," "Cabarets: A la Cabane Cubaine," Jan. 19, 1949.

AP9   "Paris Roundabout: New Films in Paris, Polish Popular Art," Feb. 2, 1949.

AP10   "Paris Roundabout," "A Note for Students," "For Dance Lovers," "Chauvin and Picabia," "Roads Out of Paris," "A Note on Tips," "To Help You Get Around Paris," March 8, 1949.

AP11   "Les Armes de la Femme," March 30, 1949.

AP12 "Art et Danses Péruviens," April 6, 1949.

AP13 "Jeanne Lafaurie," "Chez les Existentialistes," April 13, 1949.

AP14 "Carven," April 20, 1949.

AP15 "La Danse: Ballets des Champs-Élysées et Ballets Hindous," April 27, 1949.

AP16 "Paris Roundabout," "L'alpage," March 4, 1949.

AP17 "Ballet: The State of the Dance in Paris," "A Danse: Les Ballets de Monte-Carlo," "Art Galleries: The Librairie Palmes," "Saint-Germain-Des-Prés: A Legend of Youth," May 11, 1949.

AP18 "Rosario et Antonio," May 25, 1949.

AP19 "Les Ballets de Paris," June 15, 1949.

AP20 "The Dance," June 22, 1949.

AP21 "Après Carmen aux Ballets de Paris," "The Work of Roland Petit," July 6, 1949.

AP22 "La Cosmologie Poétique de Jules Supervelle," *Critique,* 38 (July 1949), 579–84.

AP23 "American Club Theater," *New York Herald Tribune,* July 20, 1949.

AP24 "Un Théâtre Américain à Paris," "Matisse," "American Club Theatre," July 20, 1949.

AP25 "Ballets de Paris," "A Real Café Concert: The Club Saint-Yves," "Chartres," July 27, 1949.

AP26 "Jeanne Lafaurie," "The Grand Ballet de Monte-Carlo," "Deauville," "Concerning Gloves . . ." "Tourism: Nice, City of Flowers," "Les Ballets de Monte-Carlo," "Air France," August 27, 1949.

AP27 "When Angels Have Cold Wings," *Continental Daily Mail,* Oct. 15, 1949.

AP28 "Katherine Dunham Au Théâtre de Paris," "Hindu Dancing," Oct. 26, 1949.

AP29 "4 Créations Aux Ballets des Champs-Élysées," "Dance Index," "Escudero, Le Maître," Nov. 23, 1949.

AP30 "The Theatre: American Club Theatre," "T.W.A.," Dec. 16, 1949.

AP31 "Le système des équivalences,'" *Combat,* March 1, 1950.

AP32 "Theatres: American Club Theatre," "Manuela del Rio," "Paris Roundabout: This is to explain Why the Left Bank Is Empty on Wednesday and Saturday Nights," April 5, 1950.

AP33   "Ballet: Térésa and Luisillo at the Sarah Bernhardt," "Teresa et Luisillo," "La Danse: Les Ballets Américains," April 26, 1950.

II. E. Michael Mendelson

Books

AP34   Los Escándalos De Maximón   1965

E. MICHAEL MENDELSON / LOS ESCANDALOS DE MAXIMON / Un estudio sobre la religión y la / visión del mundo en Santiago Atitlán / [device] / Tipografiá Nacional / Guatemala. —1965.

Pagination: pp. [1–7] 8 [9] 10–27 [28–31] 32 [33] 34–49 [50–51] 52–64 [65] 66–74 [75] 76–79 [80–81] 82–101 [102÷103] 104–119 [120–121] 122–146 [147] 148–149 [150–153] 154–166 [167] 168–186 [187] 188–201 [202–203] 204–209 [210]; 7 ¾″ × 5 7/8″; printed on wove paper.

Collation: pp. [1] title, [2] "Version Española De Julio Vielman," [3] plate, [4] blank, [5] list of consultants, [6] copyright, [7]–8 contents, [9]–27 text, [28] blank, [29] half-title, [30] blank, [31]–49 text, [50] blank, ′[51]–66 text, 67 photograph, 68–70 text, 71 text and photograph, 72–74 text, [75] photograph, 76 text, 77 photograph, 78–79 text, [80] blank, [81]–101 text, [102] blank, [103]–119 text, [120] blank, [121]–149 text, [150] blank, [151] half-title, [152] blank, [153]–170 text, 171 photograph, 172–198 text, 199 photograph, 200–201 text, [202] blank, [203]–209 text, [210] colophon.

Binding: Issued in wrappers. Front: [yellow, white, and beige background:] E. MICHAEL MENDELSON / LOS ESCANDALOS / DE MAXIMON / [mask] / Seminario de Inegración Social Guatemalteca / MINISTERIO DE EDUCATION; back: [publisher's emblem]; spine: Guatemala / 1965 [double rule] LOS ESCAN-DALOS DE MAXIMON [double rule] 19 [double rule] SEMINARIO DE / IN-TEGRACION SOCIAL / GUATEMALTECA. Front flyleaf: "Illustración de la cubierta: / Máscara de Maximón que se encuen- / tra en el Museo del Hombre, Paris."; back flyleaf: [biography of the author].

Publication: Published December 30, 1965, as Publication 19 by Seminario De Integración Social Guatemala.

Contents: "Los Escándalos de Maximón" [text in Spanish].

Note: I wrote what is referred to as "the long text" (and is available only on microfilm, not as a printed book) as my Ph.D. offering. I was shocked when I was told very late in the day that if I wanted it as a Ph.D. thesis I would have to cut it down to a hundred pages. Two things were going on there: first, there was a new tendency in the academy not to accept long theses; second, and much more important, was that Redfield wanted to put three of his students' manuscripts together and publish them as a book in world-view theory, and I was one of the three. I accepted the challenge and boiled down a text of about 600 pages to 99. This became known as the "short text." Unfortunately, Redfield had leukemia and died before he could complete the project, and no one else took it up.

When I got a proposal from the Seminario de Integración Social Guatemalteca, which was part of the Guatemalan ministry of education, that they should publish it I was glad to let them do it. It never came out in English in the end. Interestingly, the short text as published has become a kind of Guatemalan classic; it's just about impossible to go there without meeting it. All the guides who go to that village quote from it remorselessly, as a kind of folk source itself. The only parts that got into English were the various articles drawn from it.

AP35   Sangha and State in Burma   1975

Title: SANGHA AND STATE / IN BURMA / *A Study of Monastic* / *Sectarianism and Leadership* / [rule] / E. MICHAEL MENDELSON / *edited by* John P. Ferguson / *Cornell University Press* [rule] ITHACA AND LONDON

Collation: [1–7], 8–9, [10–11], 12–13, [14–15], 16–20, [21–23], 24–30, [31], 32–65, [66], 67–118, [119], 120–172, [173], 174–235, [236], 237–298, [299], 300–355, [356–358], 359, [360], 361, [362], 363, [364–367], 368, [369], 370–376, [377], 378–385, [386–387], 388–400; 9 1/8" × 6 1/4"; printed on wove paper.

Pagination: [1] half-title, [2] map, [3] title, [4] copyright, [5] dedication, [6] blank, [7]–9 contents, [10] blank, [11]–13 text, [14] blank, [15]–20 text, [21] half-title, [22] blank, [23]–355 text, [356] blank, [357] half-title, [358]–385 text, [386] blank, [387]–400 index.

Binding: Bound in blue cloth over boards. Spine: [gold-stamped:] MENDELSON / SANGHA / AND / STATE / IN / BURMA / *A Study of* / *Monastic* / *Sectarianism* / *and Leadership* / FERGUSON / EDITOR / CORNELL / UNIVERSITY / PRESS. White endpapers.

Dust jacket: Issued in yellow dust jacket, printed in blue. Front: [illustration] / SANGHA AND STATE / IN BURMA / A Study of Monastic / Sectarianism and Leadership / E. MICHAEL MENDELSON / edited by John P. Ferguson; back: [list of volumes in the "Symbol, Myth, and Ritual" series published by Cornell University Press, under general editorship of Victor Turner]; spine: [as binding]; front flyleaf: [synopsis]; back flyleaf: [brief biographies of Tarn and Ferguson].

Publication: Published by Cornell University Press on November 15, 1975, at $19.50.

Contents: Sangha and State in Burma.

Note: Although I worked on my Guatemalan project as a kind of diversion, my idea was always to go to the Far East. My first two choices were Japan and Nepal, but a lot of pressure was brought to bear on me by various people, especially my supervisor Raymond Firth at the London School of Economics. He told me that the British system needed a Burma person, and that if I went there they could find something for me to do when I got back. I didn't know anything about Burma, but I started learning both Burmese and Pali, the classical language of Burmese Buddhism. I went under the auspices of Chatham House, a British think-tank with ties to the Foreign Office. They intended for me to study the relationship between monks and politics, but when I got there I became far more interested in what I came to call "messianic Buddhism."

After ten years or more I eventually abandoned the book because of the immense difficulties I explain in the preface. Eventually, a scholar by the name of John Ferguson came to the rescue of the book, however, and as with La Légende de St. Germain-des-Prés *there is a sense in*

which this is not my book. As much as possible he was very careful to stick to the words I used, but he was cutting down from an immense manuscript and the book really emerged as a joint project. The research was so difficult that I was not paying vast attention to stylistics; rather, it came down to what I could squeeze out of myself chained to my desk, often wishing I'd never gotten started.

I was very grateful to Ferguson for saving the project because I felt guilty, given the virtual non-appearance of the Guatemalan work, at getting bogged down again. But it does seem to be the case that while there never seems to be a question in my poetry of whether something should be longer or shorter, in my scholarly prose my demon was always that I wanted to saturate meaning completely. For years I just never could control the length.

Articles

AP36   *Review:* "Mondes Africains," *Critique* (Paris), 93 (Feb., 1955), np.

AP37   *Review:* "Une Etude d'anthropologie sociale sur l'Espagne," *Critique* (Paris), 96 (May, 1955), 471–75.

AP38   *Essay:* "Past and Present Patterns of Religious and Political Organization in Highland Guatemala," *Atti dell' VIII Congresso Internazionale di storia delle religione* (Rome) (1956), 167–69.

AP39   *Essay:* "Les Indiens mayas du Guatemala," *Ici Londres,* 457 (Nov. 9, 1956), 3.

AP40   *Review:* "Les Mayas des Hautes Terres," *Critique* (Paris), 115 (Dec., 1956), 1067–87. (Reprinted in Spanish as "Los Mayas del Altiplano," Cuadernos del Seminario de Integración Social Guatemalteca, 6 (1959).

AP41   *Review:* "Indonesian Society in Transition," *Critique* (Paris), 118 (March, 1957), np.

AP42   *Review:* "A 'Stout Fighter,'" *The New Scientist,* 2, 27 (May 23, 1957), 44.

AP43   *Review:* "The Buddha and Five After Centuries," *Luzac's Oriental List* (July/Sept., 1957), np.

AP44   *Review:* "The Path of the Buddha," *Pacific Affairs,* XXX, 4 (Dec., 1957), 381–82.

AP45   *Review:* "La Nouvelle Birmanie," *Critique* (Paris), 128 (Jan., 1958), 73–85.

AP46   *Review:* "De l'Olympe à la Guinée," *Critique* (Paris), 133 (June, 1958), 541–49.

AP47   *Essay:* "The King, the Traitor, and the Cross: An Interpretation of a Highland Maya Religious Conflict," *Diogenes,* 21 (spring, 1958), 1–10. (Spanish translation in Boletín Del Instituto Indigenista Nacional, II, 1/4 (1960), 47–57.

AP48   *Essay:* "A Guatemalan Sacred Bundle," *Man,* LVII (August, 1958), 121–26.

AP49 *Essay:* "Some Present Trends of Social Anthropology in France," *The British Journal of Sociology,* IX, 3 (Sept., 1958), 251–70.

AP50 *Essay:* "Maximon: An Iconographical Introduction," *Man,* LIX (April, 1959), 57–60.

AP51 *Essay:* "A Plea for the Preservation of Buddhist Art in Burma," *The Guardian Magazine,* VI, 12 (Dec., 1959), np.

AP52 *Essay:* "Religion and Authority in Modern Burma," *The World Today,* 16, 3 (March, 1960), 110–18.

AP53 *Review:* "Sons of the Shaking Earth," *Man,* LX (Dec., 1960), 186.

AP54 *Review:* "Aspects of Caste," *International Affairs,* 37, 2 (April, 1961), 263–64.

AP55 *Essay:* "The King of the Weaving Mountain," *Royal Central Asian Journal,* XLVIII, 3/4 (July/Oct., 1961), 229–37.

AP56 *Review:* "Bali," *International Affairs,* 37, 4 (Oct., 1961), 549.

AP57 *Essay:* "A Messianic Buddhist Association in Upper Burma," *Bulletin of the School of Oriental and African Studies,* XXIV, 3 (1961), 560–80.

AP58 *Note:* "Messianic Buddhism and Political Behavior in Burma," *Abstracts of Symposium Papers, Xth Pacific Science Congress* (Hawaii), 1961, np.

AP59 *Review:* "The Virgin's Life: Life in an Aztec Village Today," *Man,* LXII (Feb., 1962), 26.

AP60 *Essay:* "Dos Oraciónes Indigenas de Santiago Atitlán," *Guatemala Indígena,* 2, 4 (Oct./Dec., 1962), np.

AP61 *Essay:* "Buddhism and Politics in Burma," *New Society,* 58 (June, 1963), 8– 10.

AP62 *Review:* "Ainu Creed and Cult," *Man,* 192 (Oct., 1963), 165.

AP63 *Letter:* "Self Sacrifice by Fire," *New Society,* 58 (Nov. 7, 1963), 41.

AP64 *Essay:* "The Uses of Religious Skepticism in Burma," *Diogenes,* 41 (1963), 94–116.

AP65 *Essay:* "Observations on a Tour in the Region of Mount Popa, Central Burma," *France-Asie* (Tokyo), XIX, 179 (1963), 780–807.

AP66 *Essay:* "Buddhism and the Burmese Establishment," *Archives De Sociologie Des Religions* (Paris), 17 (1964), 85–95.

AP67 *Review:* "Nationalism and Religion in Southeast Asia," *Pacific Affairs,* XXXVIII, 1 (spring, 1965), 64–8.

AP68   *Review:* "Road Belong Cargo," "Closed Systems and Open Minds," *The Listener,* 1900 (Aug. 26, 1965), 316.

AP69   *Essay:* "Initiation and the Paradox of Power: A Sociological Approach," *Initiation,* C.J. Bleeker, ed. Amsterdam: E.J. Brill, 1965. 214–221.

AP70   *Essay:* "Some Notes on a Sociological Approach to Gnosticism," *The Origins of Gnosticism,* Ugo Bianchi, ed. Amsterdam: E.J. Brill, 1967. 668–75.

AP71   *Essay:* "The 'Uninvited Guest': Ancilla to Lévi-Strauss on Totemism and Primitive Thought," *The Structural Study of Myth and Totemism,* Edmund Leach, ed. London: Tavistock Publications, 1967. 119–39.

AP72   *Essay:* "World View," *International Encyclopedia of the Social Sciences.* New York: Collier-Macmillan, 1967.

AP73   *Essay:* "Ritual and Mythology," *Handbook of Middle American Indians* (vol. 6). Austin: University of Texas Press, 1967. 392–415.

AP74   *Essay:* "Primitive Secret Societies," *Secret Societies,* Norman Mackenzie, ed. London: Aldus Books, 1967. 20–37.

AP75   *Essay:* "Masters of the Buddhist Occult: The Burmese Weikzas" (with John P. Ferguson), *Contributions to Asian Studies,* 16. Leiden: Brill, 1981. 62–80.

Appendix 2. Cape Editions

In 1968, Martin Seymour-Smith called Cape Editions, "perhaps the most remarkable publishing series launched since the war.... There can already be no more essential single key to the development of twentieth-century thought and letters than the collection as it now stands." Founded by Tom Maschler of Cape, with Nathaniel Tarn as general editor of the series, its first volume appeared in 1967, Claude Lévi-Strauss' *The Scope of Anthropology*. The books' format was standard — measuring 7" × 4 1/4", published in both hard and soft covers by Cape in England and Grossman in America. All were issued with dust jackets.

The aim of Cape Editions was to publish "a series of compact, elegant paperbacks of important short texts, many as yet unpublished in this country, by known and lesser-known masters. Primary, original statements in many fields will be interspersed with classic texts which need a new hearing today. The series is a meeting ground for the arts and sciences: on the one hand the poem, the essay, the play, the short story — on the other an inaugural lecture on social anthropology or a revolutionary study of animal behavior which marked the birth of the new science of comparative ethology. It is hoped that the series will encourage writers in one field to think of the others and that readers will be led from a known name to an unknown one by their trust in the high standards of selection and presentation. Cape Editions aim to close the gap between foreign and English literature by publishing works from as many languages as possible and by presenting these in rapid succession as samples of new dialogues between cultures. In this way, the series will also foster the art of translation and bring to the public a new generation of translators."

Following is a list of volumes which appeared under Tarn's general editorship. Volume 8 (Lichtenberg's *Selected Aphonisms*), although announced, was never published. Asterisks following titles indicate the volumes were proposed and acquired by Tarn himself.

AP76   *The Scope of Anthropology*, Claude Lévi-Strauss *

AP77   *Call Me Ishmael,* Charles Olson *

AP78   *Writing Degree Zero*, Roland Barthes *

AP79   *Elements of Semiology*, Roland Barthes *

AP80   *I Wanted to Write a Poem*, William Carlos Williams *

AP81   *The Memorandum*, Václav Havel

AP82   *The Selected Poems of Nazim Hikmet* *

AP83   *Tango,* Slawomir Mrozek

AP84   *On Love,* Jose Ortega y Gasset

AP85   *Manhood,* Michel Leiris *

AP86   *Bees,* Karl von Frisch *

AP87   *Lunar Caustic,* Malcolm Lowry

AP88   *Twenty Prose Poems,* Charles Baudelaire *

AP89   *Journeys,* Gunter Eich *

AP90   *A Close Watch on the Trains,* Bohumil Hrabal

AP91   *Mayan Letters,* Charles Olson *

AP92   *The Courtship Habits of the Great Crested Grebe,* Julian Huxley *

AP93   *The Supermale,* Alfred Jarry *

AP94   *Poems & Antipoems,* Nicanor Parra *

AP95   *In Praise of Krishna: Songs from the Bengali* *

AP96   *History Will Absolve Me,* Fidel Castro *

AP97   *Selected Poems,* Georg Trakl *

AP98   *Selected Poems,* Yves Bonnefoy *

AP99   *Ferdinand,* Louis Zukofsky *

AP100   *The Recluse,* Adalbert Stifter *

AP101   *Dialectical Materialism,* Henri Lefebvre *

AP102   *Soul on Ice: Selected Essays,* Eldridge Cleaver

AP103   *The Human Sciences and Philosophy,* Lucien Goldman *

AP104   *Selected Poems,* André Breton *

AP105   *Soap,* Francis Ponge *

AP106   *Histoire Extraordinaire,* Michel Butor *

AP107   *Conversations with Claude Lévi-Strauss,* G. Charbonnier *

AP108   *An Absence,* Uwe Johnson

AP109   *A Critique of Pure Tolerance,* Robert Paul Wolff, Barrington Moore Jarr, Herbert Marcuse

AP110   *The Garden Party,* Václav Havel

AP111   *Twenty Love Poems and a Song of Despair,* Pablo Neruda *

AP112   *Genesis As Myth and Other Essays,* Edmund Leach *

AP113   *Cold Mountain: 100 Poems by the T'ang Poet Han-shan* *

Note: At this point I can no longer remember whether the idea for Cape Editions came from Maschler or me. In any case, the idea was fed by similar things being done in Germany by Suhrkamp and Maspéro in Paris. The idea of a series of books with texts too long for magazine publication and too short for the conventional book was met with great enthusiasm. A series which would be multinational and interdisciplinary. This became the final reason for me leaving London University for the publishing world. I chose the first four titles myself, and in essence commissioned the first translations of Roland Barthes into English; I got my great poet father Charles Olson in there, along with my great anthropologist father Claude Lévi-Strauss, who initially was antagonistic to these sorts of projects. Subsequently, a few of the titles were not chosen by me, though eventually I agreed to them all. It was very difficult to find proper texts for this series, though for a time we were able to keep up our rhythm of about four every few months.

There was great critical attention paid to the series from the start, and even today I run across collectors of Cape Editions the way one runs across collectors of Mercedes. We had a couple of very fine unofficial advisors: Desmond Morris, who brought up the idea of the Huxley, and George Steiner.

Appendix 3. Criticism and Reviews

Criticism

AP114   Anon. "Deep Waters," *The Times Literary Supplement* (Oct. 12, 1967), np. A review of Cape's "excellent idea" in issuing "interesting and perhaps rather inaccessible texts" as Cape Editions. The issue's editorial "Filtering Through" comments on "an enlightened new series of paperbacks" as one possible cross-cultural channel of communication.

AP115   Anon. "Fresh Bookmaking Ideas in Private Press' Poetry Series," *Publisher's Weekly* (July 1, 1968), 76–7. Describes the setting up of Cape-Goliard Press and its work to date. Three books are photographed, including the title page and "The Laurel Tree" page from *Where Babylon Ends,* and that book is described in some detail.

AP116   Anon. *The Transmedia Newsletter* 2 (Jan., 1969), 1–2. In a study of publishers who have apparently chosen literary over commercial values, the article reviews the history of Cape Editions in the hand of Tarn; its enthusiastic reception by David Daiches, George Steiner, Frank Kermode, John Berger, Martin Seymour-Smith, and others; the benefits to Cape and Cape Editions' dismissal of Tarn "for purely commercial reasons" — a sad prospect whether the series survives in a maimed form or is discontinued.

AP117   Burgess, Anthony. "Short Sharp Stimulants," *The Sunday Times* (Oct. 8, 1967), 3. In this review of the first four Cape Editions, Burgess describes "an important publishing event. It's a gesture of faith in concision and a repudiation of the heresy — as common among publishers as readers — that length can be equated with value . . . We shall be able to carry intellectual stimulation about like a pocket transistor."

AP118   Carmack, Robert. *Quichean Civilization.* Berkeley: University of California Press, 1973; 253. "Throughout his monograph, Mendelson focuses on ritual and belief associated with confradia, and in untangling the symbolic themes used in these rituals he sheds considerable light on aboriginal ethics and mythology. We can only imagine the cultural historical possibilities had he paid more attention to native language and social organization in the process of obtaining data for his ingenious analysis."

AP119   Corngold, Stanley. "*Where Babylon Ends:* Nathaniel Tarn's Poetic Development," *Boundary 2,* IV, 1 (fall, 1975), 57–75. A general discussion of Tarn's work through *Babylon,* including comments on "the scope of the early work" (wherein

"Tarn has constructed a complex and luminous cosmos turning around his own invisibility"), narration, and figurative language. *Babylon* itself "radicalizes the conflict of the claims of mimetic and allegorical language in favor of allegory . . . The lyricism founded on the myth of the one true empirical personality is abandoned for the dramatic mode of many voices."

AP120   Etchells, D.R. *The Man with the Trumpet: Some Mid-Century English Writing.* London: Longman, 1970; 155–57. Reprints "Where Babylon Ends," noting that the poem "uses traditional Hebrew symbols to express a hope for the future . . . 'Babylon' is the future, waiting for Godot, waiting for "reprieve."

AP121   Felstiner, John. "Neruda in Translation," *The Yale Review* (winter, 1972), 226–51. Tarn's *Macchu Picchu* "takes a number of dramatic risks, some successful, some not, and provides a strong, at times memorable, reading."

AP122   Fisch, Harold. "Nathaniel Tarn and A.M. Klein: Poets of the Hebraic Consciousness," *Judaism,* 14, 4 (fall, 1965), 479–90. "For all his Jewish allusiveness, his Hebrew and Jewish background is fairly tenuous . . . Yet, as Tarn comes to remind us, the Jewish poet is not exempt from inward questioning, that struggle for significance amid the darkness of unanswered riddles."

AP123   Fisch, Harold. *The Dual Image: The Figure of the Jew in English and American Literature.* London: World Jewish Library, 1971; 109–10. In this study of the Jew in literature from the Middle Ages to the present, Fisch mentions Tarn's "kabbalistically inspired poems" which "combine images of Auschwitz with messianic fantasies."

AP124   Giordano, Fedora. "Il Mito come Metalinguaggio nella Poesia di Nathaniel Tarn," *Letteratura d'America* (Rome), V, 22 (spring, 1984), 95–126. A long and detailed study, the first in any language (here Italian), of *Lyrics for the Bride of God,* using the Rasula/Erwin interview, Tarn's "Heraldic Vision" essay, etc. "Lyrics . . . locates itself in the poetic tradition which, from Whitman to Williams, Pound and Olson, sees the writing of an American poem as a recreation of America. To vivify his scope, Tarn has recourse to esoteric traditions, Jung, Maya, Greek and Hebraic mythology, creating a multi-cultural poem which is both a reflection on poetic language and an autobiographical meditation. For Tarn is a European expatriate who has taken America as his chosen, elected land . . . Already, in *The Beautiful Contradictions,* Tarn had privileged the use of fragments by introducing four major cultural components: Maya, Buddhist, Hebraic, and the contemporary world. One of the poetic 'contradictions' was present in the mode of composition — that of collage. To the feminine was ascribed the role of symbolizing the element of Time. The poet's struggle within two contradictory conceptions of Time: the linear and the circular worked toward a resolution with the introduction of the Kabbalistic figure of the Female Aspect of God, the Shekhinah, unifier of opposites, conciliator of synchrony and diachrony." A rich analysis of various sections of *Lyrics* follows.

AP125   Glanville, Brian. "Nathaniel Tarn: Poetry and the Cabala," *Jewish Chronicle* (March 13, 1964), np. Tarn "is a Jewish poet who, in some of his work, makes use of the Cabala." Includes quotations from interview with Tarn on Judaism.

AP126   Harrop, Dorothy A. "Craft Binders at Work XI: Sally Lou Smith," *The Book Collector,* 30, 3 (autumn, 1981), 315–34. A discussion of the binding work of Sally

Lou Smith, with mention of *The Forest* and full-page reproduction of the book's binding.

AP127   Howard, Michael S. *Jonathan Cape: Publisher.* London: Jonathan Cape, 1971. A biography of Jonathan Cape, which devotes a few pages to Tarn's association with Cape Goliard. "Tarn conceived the notion of a little press within the framework of an established house ... Tarn's wide interests and his ideal of bridging literary disciplines" were at the center of the Cape Editions project.

AP128   Kermode, Frank. "In Parvo," *The Listener* (Oct. 12, 1967), np. In a review of the first four Cape Editions, "that extraordinary little batch of books," the venture is described as "a series bolder, more extreme in its demands on the reader, closer to high intellectual fashion, than any since the war. They make a striking, and incidentally a physically handsome quartet ... The venture deserves unqualified support, like buying the books."

AP129   Lenfest, David S. "Notes Toward a Study of Nathaniel Tarn's *The Beautiful Contradictions,* The Poetry of Material Transmigration," *Boundary 2,* IV, 1 (fall, 1975), 77–95. Tarn's method is "the Hegelian process of thesis, antithesis, and synthesis." A close reading of *Contradictions,* a poem whose central metaphor "returns to archetypal women; it "constitutes a poetic foundation" for the poet in America, "with America as a center."

AP130   P.P.S., "The Times Diary," *The Times* (July 12, 1967), 8. Announces the creation of the Cape-Goliard Press, quotes an interview with Tarn, and gives some publication data and figures.

AP131   "Pooter." *The Times Saturday Review* (Jan. 31, 1970), np. Pointedly and outspokenly reviews the details of Tarn's departure from Jonathan Cape and England itself. The "poet/anthropologist with a certain title to grey eminence himself" tells the story of his disappointment with "Little Englandism" in poetry, publishing, and the universities, and is described as leaving England as a "deflated emigrant to Princeton." In a refutation (*The Times,* Feb. 10, 1970), Tarn contests the "deflation" and expresses pleasure in his Princeton appointment.

AP132   Ratner, Rochelle. "Poetry," *The Soho Weekly News* (Nov. 4, 1976), 27. A brief discussion of the Tarn/Rodney in progress *Alashka:* "The poem seems to be happening on three different levels — the anticipatory level, the present, and the retrospective."

AP133   Redfield, Robert. *Human Nature and the Study of Society* (Collected Papers, vol. 1). Chicago: University of Chicago Press, 1962. 280-1, 400-1. After quoting a letter of field instructions to Mendelson of August 22, 1952, account is given of Mendelson's analysis of worldview in Santiago Atitlán, Guatemala. "For me this case helps to continue a progression, a progression in the development of world views as structures or systems more or less simple or complex, shallow or provided with perspective, coherent or incoherent, separated or unified, held in unconflicting integrity or split and held in tension."

AP134   Russell, Peter. "Letter from Europe," *Transition* (Kampala), VI, 17 (1969), 47–52. Reviewing the 1964 Berlin Conference of Poets, and Tarn's "particularly interesting paper" on Poetry and Communication: "I cannot leave it without remarking that Tarn, though more than usually versed in science and philosophy, certainly did not fall into . . . the trap of thinking that the whites' culture was 'all intellect and machine.' Unlike the pop artists and trivial University poets who are all the rage today (in England at least) he affirmed in no uncertain voice the traditional themes of the poetry of our ancestors, 'this original voice . . . where we come from and where we go and what it is we are doing here.'"

AP135   Sanesi, Robert. "Primi appunti sulla tematica di *The Beautiful Contradictions*," in *Le Belle Contradizzioni* [Italian translation of *BC*]. Milan: Munt Press, 1973; 101–05. "*The Beautiful Contradictions* seems to me to be one of the most significant and complex attempts at global poetry since *The Waste Land* . . . A text of wide, severe, homogeneous rhythm, founded primarily on ideas, dedicated to the dialectical resolution of an arduous problematic, indifferent in the end to descriptive temptations yet not backing off from using references of a varied nature, recalling into play the structural elements and signification of poetic 'making,' insisting on its inevitable internationality and atemporality while keeping a firm grip on contemporary data." A thematic analysis of the poem, section by section.

AP136   Seymour-Smith, Martin. "Cape of Good Hope," *Spectator* (Dec. 13, 1968), 849–50. "Cape editions, perhaps the most remarkable publishing series launched since the war, has now reached its twenty-sixth volume. There can already be no more essential single key to the development of twentieth-century thought and letters than the collection as it stands." Continues with a discussion of the Series, and Tarn's contribution as General Editor.

AP137   Seymour-Smith, Martin. "Nathaniel Tarn," *Contemporary Poets*. New York: St. Martins, 1970. Tarn's poetry is "the most non-traditional and foreign-influenced of any British poet now writing," in which the influences of Lévi-Strauss, Neruda, and Oriental thought are detected. The work is "difficult," "sprawling," with a "remarkably consistent range of metaphor and imagery," and totally eschews "the false neatness of the traditional English-language poem." Examines books from *Old Savage/Young City* to *The Beautiful Contradictions*.

AP138   Sommer, Doris. "America as Desire(d): Nathaniel Tarn's Poetry of the Outsider as Insider," *American Poetry*, 2, 1 (fall, 1984), 13–35. "Of the various strategies that Tarn came upon for negotiating a peace between Jekyll and Hyde [the anthropologist and the poet], desire and fulfillment, the happiest was to come to America . . . Tarn's poetry is pitched to intelligent, somewhat jaded readers whom it manages to outstrip with a verbal and allusive density that puts the erudition of an accomplished ethnographer at the reach of the common, but careful, reader."

AP139   Weinberger, Eliot. "Nathaniel Tarn," *Contemporary Poets*. New York: St. Martins, 1986. This review-article examines the "range of Tarn's" work over a complex multi-disciplinary career. "What holds it together is Tarn's extatic [sic] vision, his continuing enthusiasm for the stuff of the world. It is a poetry whose native tongue is myth and it rolls out in long lines of sacred hymns that o[s]cillate between the demotic and the hieratic (heir to Smart and Blake, to Whitman and Neruda . . .) and sequences of short poems, small linked bursts of sharp image and speech, which tie Tarn to Williams and contemporary practitioners like Snyder and Kelly. Since the death of Rexroth, he is the major celebrant of heterosexual love in the language. His combination of ingenious metaphor and sexual exuberance has not been heard in English since the 17th century."

Selected Reviews

Old Savage / Young City
AP140   John Smith, *Poetry Review* (autumn, 1964), 55:167. The book is the editor's choice for the period. "A full, rich, and outstanding book. He makes a serious attempt to reveal the essence of things and to explore man's spiritual predicament."

AP141   Zulfikar Ghose, *Western Mail* (Nov. 26, 1964), np. "One hears Eliot's rhythms in this and some other poems, but for sheer rhetorical punch and intellectual toughness Tarn's is a new and original voice."

AP142   P.N. Furbank, *The Listener* (Dec. 10, 1964), 72:949. Furbank does not "much like Nathaniel Tarn's poems." He finds them "voluble and dazzling," but also "a bit easy and a bit false": "showy metaphors," "false brilliance," "approximate effect."

AP143   A. Alvarez, *The Observer Weekend Review* (Dec. 20, 1964), 17. "A serious writer, full of good will, decency and right feeling. But his emotions, though large, seem vague and curiously imprecise . . . 'The Delivery' is almost fine and certainly ambitious . . . As yet, he cannot quite give flesh to his half-realised dream of a big, moving poem."

AP144   Elizabeth Jennings, *The Spectator* (Jan. 1, 1965), 22. "Taut and virile"; a breaking away from "a small concern with self and over-regular forms . . . This is a very fine, vigorous first book."

AP145   John Fuller, *The Guardian* (Jan. 1, 1965), np. The author is a "biblical tub-thumper" who can be "sharp and inventive" but eventually wearies the reader with his "verbosity."

AP146   Anon., *The Times Literary Supplement* (Jan. 7, 1965), 10. "His style is a very original mixture of the high and the low, the deliberately elevated and the humorously familiar, like Whitman's own style. It has a remarkable if sometimes too deliberate muscularity."

AP147   Danny Abse, *Jewish Chronicle* (Jan. 15, 1965), 25. Despite much "non-poetic abstruseness and empty rhetoric," the book is very ambitious, "excited and exciting," "haunting," "compassionate," frequently justifying the erudition. "A truly interesting poet has arrived upon the scene."

AP148   Christopher Ricks, *The New Statesman* (Jan. 15, 1965), 69:79. The poems are "grandiloquent . . . There are many big words, but all they do is flex themselves."

AP149   Martin Seymour-Smith, *The Scotsman* (Jan. 30, 1965), np. Notes the poet's "very long lines" and rhythms "which have no recognizable relation to any known rhythms of the past." The poems are "insidiously exciting."

AP150   Cyril Connolly, *The Sunday Times* (Jan. 31, 1965), 47. The poetry of this first book is "rather amorphous . . . His awareness of his Jewish ancestry orientates eastwards, as in the unusual and moving 'René Grousset Weeping at the Doors of the Shosoin.'"

AP151   Seamus Heaney, *Vogue* [London] (June, 1965), 51. "Unpredictable subject-matter, extravagent [sic] imaginative take-offs and skillfully controlled landings will commend this complex and sometimes fantastic verse to those who prefer oblique suggestion to direct statement."

AP152   Paul Thompson, *Sunday Denver Post* (June 13, 1965), np. "An authentic poet" with "strikingly bold, brilliantly cohesive imagery." The poems "show careful workmanship and an acceptance of the world remarkably free from bitterness."

AP153   George Scarbrough, *Chattanooga Times* (June 27, 1965), 23. An originality rarely seen in recent verse, "fresh and invigorating . . . sometimes sounding like a language of the future."

AP154   Anon., *King Features Syndicate* (June 30, 1965), np. The work is distinguished "by a complete mastery of language used with compressive dynamism, a perfect sense of meter and a toughness which is the result of competent craftsmanship." Other poets should study his discipline, a quality more and more ignored.

AP155   X.J. Kennedy, *The New York Times* (Sept. 25, 1966), 18. Tarn is a good poet with "several near-brilliant successes" which nevertheless "make one wonder at the over-all grayness of this first collection . . . Too many poems end in questions and tentatives . . . waver between flatness and hyperbole."

AP156   Winfield T. Scott, *Saturday Review* (Oct. 9, 1965), 48:58. "A poet with real vitality . . . a direct language which makes its effect not by tricks but by emotional force. The verse is sometimes loose or too conversational . . . sometimes manages well the long line."

Los Escándalos de Maximón
AP157   S. Ortiz, *Man: Journal of the Royal Anthropological Institute* (March, 1967), II, 1:149. While she finds some of the presentation methods confusing, Ortiz sees the book as an interesting attempt to interpret Atiteco worldview through the complex figure of the Maximón icon and deplores the fact that the book only exists in Spanish.

Penguin Modern Poets 7
AP158   Elizabeth Jennings, *The Daily Telegraph* (March 24, 1966), np. The reviewer is surprised not to find Tarn in Alvarez's *The New Poetry*. "For Mr. Tarn words come, as they do with Lawrence and Dylan Thomas, welling straight out of experience, though his work has more intellectual content than that of either of the other two poets."

AP159   Christopher Ricks, *The Sunday Times Magazine* (Aug. 21, 1966), 34. "Not at all a poet for me — exclamatory, dark, Biblical, with much talk of thighs and bones and wombs . . . Tarn is, it seems, a pseudonym; it is also an anagram for rant."

Pablo Neruda: The Heights of Macchu Picchu

AP160   Anselm Hollo, *International Times* (Jan. 16–29, 1967), 14. Hollo finds Neruda's imagery to be "essentially Victorian, decorative, feeble in a flashy way." Tarn's effort to find an idiom equivalent to "these perfumed symboliste meanderings is an honorable one," but he does not attempt to transform *Macchu Picchu* into a great English poem.

AP161   Anon., *The Times Literary Supplement* (March 16, 1967), 4. The title of the piece gives the tone: "Tarnished Neruda." Tarn's "clumsy rendering is neither acceptable as English nor particularly accurate." The translation is "arbitrarily interpretive — most impudently so when [Tarn] takes it upon himself to infest the poem with Christian associations wholly absent in the original."

AP162   Dudley Fitts, *The New York Times Book Review* (May 21, 1967), 6. Despite almost insoluble obstacles, Tarn has given a largely faithful rendering. His poem, though not Neruda's, "is a poem, frequently an impressive one, in its own right" and should give "some idea of the quality of the original." Fitts cites lapses, though Tarn "has served his audience and Pablo Neruda generously and well."

AP163   Anon., *The Kirkus Service* (March 15, 1967), np. "A rare experience" in a "fine" and "excellent" translation which "succeeds in conveying and sharpening the quality of the poetry, although it occasionally substitutes more highly colored words for the original vocabulary."

AP164   M.L. Rosenthal, *Saturday Review* (Sept. 2, 1967), 25. "Tarn's translation is conscientious and suggestive, misses some of the rhythmic and echoing cues and too often sacrifices a chance to evoke the sound and syntax of the original. It does, though, catch the luxuriant ambiguity, the delicate exploration, and the power of many passages."

AP165   Ralph J. Mills, *Modern Age* (fall, 1967), 439. The Tarn version is "a very readable and moving poem in English" which "has rendered readers who know little or no Spanish . . . a genuine service."

AP166   Anon., *Virginia Quarterly* (autumn, 1967), 172. Tarn, a "poet of great ability," has given an "excellent translation"; provides "a brilliant beginning into a full understanding" of this important poet.

AP167   James Wright, *Poetry* (June, 1968), 112,3:191–4. "Although personally I would hem and haw over this and that detail of Mr. Tarn's translation, I have to confess that I think it is a beautiful poem in the English language, worthy of noble and spacious poem which identifies Neruda as one of the precious few great masters of our time and of any time."

Where Babylon Ends

AP168   Richard Holmes, *The Times Saturday Review* (April 6, 1968), 20. Holmes notes Tarn's "distinguished translation" of Neruda, interest in myth, anthropology, and Black Mountain poets. "The poetry is hard to grasp, grand and yet muffled. But he is alone in England on this new frontier (as starkly as that), and we must wait and see."

AP169   Anon., *The Times Literary Supplement* (May 16, 1968), 499. The poems are "uncompromisingly creatures of the page" and are not free of "pretentiousness." But "the dense feral metaphors suggest at least some inner obsessional need, though its project is as much modish as magical."

Selected Poems of Kenneth Patchen
AP170   Miles, *International Times* (July 26/ Aug. 8, 1968), 36:17. "Large, beautifully produced and carefully edited, this book represents the 'best buy' of all Patchen's books ... Tarn's selection, though a very personal one, is wide-ranging and representative." Suggests Cape should provide Britain with Patchen's picture-poems.

The Beautiful Contradictions
AP171   Richard Holmes, *The Times Saturday Review* (June 7, 1969), 20. Tarn desires "an encircling of all human conditions with imagination" and "at once the largeness, the confidence is striking ... His weapon is anthropology." Tarn uses myth "as a visionary expression and solution of social contradictions." Holmes notes influences from Lévi-Strauss, Neruda, and Breton. "Beyond anything, the risk is magnificent because it is the genuine alternative, a poetry of exploration."

AP172   Jeremy Robson, *Tribune* (Aug. 8, 1969), 11. "A long and ambitious poem, by turns pontifical, rhetorical, maddeningly esoteric ... yet it is an energetic, sometimes moving work, an arresting cross-fertilization of Eliot and Neruda." Tarn shows courage in taking risks and the "visionary passages" vindicate him.

AP173   Anon., *The Times Literary Supplement* (Aug. 14, 1969), 898. A "strenuous quest produces a laughably bad book." The language is "vapid." This "is a poetry of a man who has come through a tremendous foreign reading list and lived to get it all mixed up for us."

AP174   Robert Nye, *The Birmingham Post* (Sept. 8, 1969), np. An extension of range, loosening of the line, and more direct speech. Sometimes encyclopaedic like MacDiarmid but "for the most part, he is persuasive and exact, and there is an unmistakeable nobility inherent in his intent." An unusual voice, "Tarn seems to me to have more potential than most poets now writing."

AP175   John Frow, *The Canberra Times* (Oct. 14, 1969), 23. Sees Olson's influence, at work in "Where Babylon Ends," as coming to fruition in this book. Notes the influence of ritual ("Tarn is an anthropologist") in mediating between past, present, and future; leads to Tarn's concern with "a radical politics of renewal and revolution" which can also be seen "as a form of dynamic conservation." Despite some prosaic passages, Tarn "is one of the best poets now writing in English."

AP176   Patrick J. Callahan, *Poet Lore* (autumn, 1971), 66, 3:317–19. In this "book-length poem of unusual power and intellectual substance," Tarn "does no less than propose a model for the restructuring of twentieth-century culture." The poem's major themes are outlined.

Pablo Neruda: Selected Poems
AP177   Alexander Coleman, *New York Times Book Review* (May 7, 1972), 4. Reviewing Bly and Tarn anthologies as products of a post–Belitt era, "the Tarn volume is especially useful; it is a lovely book and contains a generous, even sumptuous, selection from all of Neruda's major phases." [On June 4, 1972, the *NYTBR* chose the book as one of the five best of the year].

AP178   Robert Bly, *Review* (fall, 1972), 6:65. The review is dominated by Bly's opinion that the "language the English use is too colorless these days to translate Neruda." He reviews the various translators' strengths and weaknesses, concluding that the collection is "a good job on the whole."

A Nowhere for Vallejo

AP179   Herbert C. Burke, *Library Journal* (April 15, 1971), 96:1373. Burke detects the presence of Olson's "projectivist, humanist, nonracist traditions" in the title poem, whose major themes are outlined. The "three groups of splendid poems" belong in any library.

AP180   Elizabeth Jennings, *The Scotsman* (Feb. 9, 1972), 23. The title poem "has much of the scope and depth of perception of some of the 'Cantos,'" moving along with "conviction," "excitement," and "ease," "firm but not obvious music," a rare capacity to make the past "not only vibrant, but immediate . . . His book is a major achievement."

AP181   Lyman Andrews, *The Sunday Times* (Sept. 3, 1972), 2. Tarn "continues in his new vein (first seen in 'October') . . . Admirers of the earlier volume from Trigram should definitely read this, where that fine sequence appears in context."

AP182   Peter Porter, *The Guardian* (Sept. 14, 1972), np. Porter is so obsessed with Tarn's departure for "the subsidised lushness of the United States poetry world" that it becomes for him the book's subject. The technique is "prodigious" but the ear is "too fashionable . . . A number of finely wrought passages" are offset by too much "gilding."

Lyrics for the Bride of God

AP183   Helen Vendler, *The New York Times Book Review* (Sept. 7, 1975), 6–18. "The pretentious are always with us, this time in the persons of the (pseudonymous) Nathaniel Tarn and David Slavitt. Tarn, who in middle age has found a new girl, writes poems to her entitled 'Lyrics for the Bride of God,' which makes Tarn, you guessed it, God. It is a book to make one regret that Ezra Pound ever wrote, and that Olson followed him. Tarn's lines are an unspeakable mixture of myth and biology, with some modern stuff thrown in after the manner of 'Paterson,' and a running allegory with La Traviata added for good measure. Someone at New Directions must have turned down some other manuscript so as to print these awful verses. Here at random, an excerpt from what they like these days at New Directions . . ." This review was answered by the managing editor of Doubleday (*New York Times,* Sept. 28, 1975), Daniel Halpern (*American Poetry Review,* Sept./Oct., 1975), and Rochelle Ratner (*The Soho Weekly News,* Oct. 2, 1975).

AP184   Louis Sasso, *Library Journal* (Sept. 15, 1975), 1636. The poem "in the line of Pound's *Cantos* and Olson's *Maximus* . . . is a dense, tough, unrelenting work of self-exploration, a form of catharsis, but one in which the poet never loses control." It is full of "honesty and directness."

AP185   Hayden Carruth, *Harpers Bookletter* (Oct. 13, 1975), 2, 5:13. The poem celebrates the mythical eternal female and studies the modern sexual dilemma in a verse style "allusive and complex . . . levying upon the whole battery of poetic devices to attain pace, variety, and power." What is attempted "is a poem in the grand modern manner, after Pound's *Cantos* or Williams' *Paterson,*" and Tarn "has largely succeeded."

AP186   Anon., *San Francisco Review of Books* (Oct., 1975), I, 6:23. "Sometimes far too wordy and certainly demanding, the work stands as a man's profound exploration of androgyny and change."

AP187   Anon., *Choice* (Nov., 1975), 204–5. "At times, he sounds distinctly like Whitman, a Whitman writing about America in the 1970's. But his style is strikingly different and idiosyncratic . . . Tarn is both brilliant and exasperating; nonetheless this work is eminently rewarding."

The House of Leaves
AP188   D.M. Thomas, *The Times Literary Supplement* (May 20, 1977), 616. Tarn has adopted America since 1970 and this book "is a little like flying over America" in its "expansiveness" and "continental ambition." Despite much repetition, "much of it is beautiful and true" and "the trip is richer and better value than most of our English suburban train-rides."

AP189   A. Kingsley Weatherhead, *Credences* (1977), 4:30–35. Charts the course, through several books, of the poet's Americanization. With many quotations, Weatherhead treats locale, space, the "primitive," myth and oracle, the feminine as medium to the adoption of a continent, and the house as microcosm of the "hidden kingdom."

Sangha and State in Modern Burma
AP190   Charles F. Keyes, *Journal of Asian Studies* (Nov., 1976), XXXVI, 1:183–4. Mendelson's "major work" studies "the relationship between Sangha and State in Burma," greatly advancing "our understanding of the Sangha as an actual social entity, distinct from the Sangha as an idealized institution." This "excellent framework" makes one "grateful" and wish for more.

AP191   B.R. Pearn, *Asian Affairs* (Oct., 1976), np. An "illuminating work . . . the fruit of careful study during an extensive period in Burma" by an "experienced anthropologist"—but only part of a "massive study" of monastic organization, messianism and animism in Burma. "A vast amount of information of a highly detailed character" will be of "high value" to the specialist rather than the general reader.

AP192   Trevor Ling, *The Times Higher Education Supplement* (Dec. 17, 1976), 16. "A pioneer in the field" of the study of folk elements in Buddhism, the book provides "a valuable corrective" to previous studies of the Burmese Sangha. "On every count, Mendelson's work must rank as one of the most important works on Burmese Buddhism that has yet been published."

AP193   Melford E. Spiro, *American Anthropologist* (1977), 79:270–1. Despite its incompleteness, Mendelson, "perhaps the foremost Western expert on esoteric Buddhism," has provided an "indispensable work" on the organization of the Buddhist monkhood in Burma.

AP194   Michael Carrithers, *Modern Asian Studies* (July, 1977), 11,3:476–79. Mendelson's work "will remain standard reading" in that field, persisting·as it does "in asking relevant questions." Its "deft use of documentary material should stand as a model to anthropologists working in literate societies." Despite a perhaps over-political view of the Sangha and a need for greater attention to Pali learning, Mendelson's understanding of Buddhist doctrine is "sound and trustworthy."

Atitlán/Alashka
AP195   Andrew Hope, *Neek: News of the Sitka Native Community* (Jan., 1980), 3.
Hope refuses the universalism implicit in the work and explores issues connected with
regionalism and Alaskans' refusal to consider the poem "Alashka." He insists on
describing Janet Rodney as Tarn's "silent partner."

AP196   Richard Dauenhauer, *World Literature Today* (summer, 1980), np. An expert in oral literature, Dauenhauer identifies the main themes of the book: life,
language, love and literature, and the integration of these in an interpretation of the
poet's place in the natural and cultural world. Noting problems in inter-ethnic communication, he finds these "admirably handled but not satisfactorily resolved" in
"Alashka," though not through any fault of the poets.

AP197   Rochelle Ratner, *American Book Review* (July/Aug., 1980), 2:14. Ratner
examines the early "anthropological" poetry in terms of attempts to create a world-
view, a politics internationalist and feminist, and a history of the American continent. She writes of mastery of "the longist narrative poem" — Olsonian process and
the "complete vision" of each succeeding book. While the publication of "Alashka"
with earlier poems makes sense in Tarnian terms, it detracts somewhat from the im-
portance of Rodney's own voice. Nevertheless, "'Alashka' is a true collaboration,
male and female writing as one, calling into being that hermaphrodite which Tarn
envisioned in his earliest work."

AP198   Theodore Enslin, *American Book Review* (July/Aug., 1980), 2:15. "In this
handsome book . . . it becomes clear what the full range of Tarn's interest may en-
compass, and how an omnivorous appetite is controlled by a discriminating intelli-
gence, at the same time that the rush of highly colored and charged language fills the
landscape with both form and the form's detail. And it is an actual landscape — the
landscape of the American hemisphere." Enslin dwells on the moral intent of the
travelogue and the "misery of the soul" and "whole-souled outrage" of the poem at
what man has made of this land.

AP199   Ian Robinson, *Shearsman* (1982), 5:82–6. This "great poet" has found a
new subject matter in anthropology, one "that would not be personally limiting, and
yet would be culturally extensive," as well as a new language in which to express it.
By assimilating the data and the methods of science, technology, and history to his
own imaginative legacy, Tarn has raised profound questions on the nature and concerns of poetry which stand in stark contrast to English production today.

The Desert Mothers, At the Western Gates
AP200   George Economou, *Sulfur* (1985), 14:167–73. This review-article examines Tarn's statement that the poet forms "a world-model, a cosmic model for
himself, which he then localizes or universalizes according to need." The poet's "emotional intensity" and "notable intellectual breath" are put to serve analysis of macro-
cosm/microcosm relations. Even in short lyrics, an epic vision is maintained. While
Western Gates relates mainly to communion with nature, *Desert Mothers'* poems "are
unified in their emphasis on Tarn's citizenship in the community of poets and artistic
innovators." Economou stresses particularly Tarn's recognition and tapping of "his
own feminine/maternal sources" in order to commune with nature and revive the fail-
ing human city.

AP201   Gene Frumkin, *Artspace* (1985-6), X, 1:57–8. Frumkin places "this Paris-
born, British-raised anthropologist of religion among the most authentically thought-

ful and daring poets living in America today." He examines the research the poems carry out into the sacred in terms of binary oppositions between self-possession and ideal marriage; the desert as killer and birther; migration West and death in the East of the old civilizations. Tarn's lyricism is "the music of mind's flow through the mystery of nature."

AP202   Geoffrey O'Brien, *The Village Voice Literary Supplement* (Feb., 1986), 18. While poetry is narrowing its concerns, Tarn "risks a scale epic enough to contain mountains and oceans . . . Tarn keeps his lines of communication open to more than one life form; with a prophetic sureness of direction, his new poems move beyond their surface splendor into the depths beneath."

Title Index

A

Abulafia at the Gates of Rome, A.D. 1280 A1, C15
Accidents A10, C94, C95
Adam Pacific A1, C10
Afrasian B3
After Jouve A17
After the Roaring Forties A4, D57
Afterword A10
Aging Hands A10, C103, E24
Airline for Ariadne A17, C121
Alashka C158
Alaskan Artists of the World Unite C144
All These Shitty Little Places in New Jersey C201
America A14, C118
American Ann A19
Americans in Paris C194
Amor Americano C101
Anatomie de la 'Pop culture' C26
And Even the Republic Must Have an End C180
Angleterre's s'interroge C18
Animal Bride A27, C192
Anniversary A17
Annunciation C15
Anton Bruckner A17, C106
Antonin Artaud A16, A17
Apparition A10
Arahiyama C14
Archeology C163
Archeology, Elegy, Architecture C176
The Arrival A14
Art Far from Us C105
Art in an African Society C73
At a Meeting, the Cry C191

At Gloucester, Mass. E26, E36
At the Western Gates A28
Atitlan/Alashka A23
Atlantis: An Anthropology C139
The Aura A19, C129

B

Baptizing Masai A2, A3, C48, E3
The Bay Dies of Pollution and Decoys Rise in Price A27, C193
The Beaches A17, C94
The Beautiful Contradictions A6
Beautiful Contradictions A6, A23, E12, E17, E20, E23, E32, E36, E42, E43
Berliner Festwochen C35
Between Delaware and Hudson A17, C166
Bicentennial Ode A23
Birdscapes, with Seaside A21
Black Mountain C156
Blackfly Melting A1, A22
Blood Bank I A23
Blood Bank II A23
Brevet D16
Bring a Child Flowers A1, A3, A22, E22
Burial, San Pedro Chenalho C17

C

Cancionero De Abajo D13
Cancionero Del Clara Palacio D13

119

Canciones Sin Su Musica D13
Cemetary at Vilcashuamen D4
The Child as Father to Man in the
American Uni-Verse C196
Children of a More Generous World A29
Choices A10, A23, C95
The Church, Santiago A17
Cities A23, C155
Cliffs of the Ultimate Record C191
The College A17, C143
Companion for Bohemia C45
Con Cuba B4
Concert A9, C83
Concorde B8
Connie Burrows A17
The Cranes A17
The Creature A19, C126
Le 'Cri du coeur' d'Ewart Milne C23
Cuban Verse D7
Cultural Ripoff C154
The Cure A1, A3, C13, C52, E2, E9
The Curtains A10

D

The Damaske Rose E30
The Dark Night A10
Das Leben das wir nicht fuhren C39
De Las Furias y Las Penas D11
Death Fear—Yet of Another A27,
C192
The Delivery A1, A3, C15
A Departure A26
Desde Pachichyut A17, C165, E41
The Desert Mothers A27
The Dictator A14
Discussion C71
Dispersal A2, A3, C42, C43
Dr. Jekyll, the Anthropologist
Emerges C197
Dog Viewing Deer C190
The Dream A23

E

Eagle at Bookfair C44
Eagle Hunt, Hidasta Indians, U.S.A.

A4, E4
The Eagles of Rome C47
Earth-Till A19, C132, C135
The Eden Foxes A1, A3, A20
Eight from Hokkaido C173
El Golpe Avisa D19
El ser que yo amo me pega D15
El tiena un planta azul D15
Elegant for Whom? C70
Elizavine of Elliotte C84
Ely Cathedral A1, A3, C19, E1
Energetically Singing Against Vora-
cious Earth C180
Enlarging Our Horizons C34
Entering Into This A27, C192
Los Escándalos De Maximón AP34
Ethnographies C203
Eyes Alone with Their Shadows C182,
C183
Eyes Watching Up-Sky C187

F

The Female Aspect of God C92
The Field of Merit A10
The Fineries A1, C30
The Fire Poem A17, C134, C138
First Cardinal A17, C121
The First Men A23
The Five Senses A4
Flight from the Mountaintop A27,
C172, C178, C181
The Floating Life C36
Food A17, C141
For a New Realism A10
For Buffy Sainte-Marie A10, A11,
C95, C96, E15
For Louis Brunel's Chambermaid E5
For Mahler A4, C64
For the Death of Anton Webern Par-
ticularly A1, A3, A21, E6
For the Rules of Flight A27, C186
For Those in Washington C120
For Toby Olson C164
The Forest A22, A23
Fossil Song A19, C129
Fountains Abbey Under Snow A1, E2
Fragments from the Prayers A23,
C89, E39

Fresh Frozen Fenix C198
From Anthropologist to Informant
    C113
From the Mercer Museum's Windows
    C191
From the Point of View of Anchises
    C118
Further Annotations from Baja
    California A28

G

The Gate of Esperaunce A19, C133
Giovanni di Paolo on Parade in New
    York City C84
Girl from Another Tribe A19
Girl in Soup A19
Gisants D21
The Going of All Dogs C184
Going Through Gates A23
The Great Odor of Summer A10,
    A23, C86, C87
*The Ground of Our Great Admiration of
    Nature* A20, A23, C166

H

Hamma Hamma City A23
Hans Memling C199
*He Who Hunted Birds in His Father's
    Village* B9
A Head with a Lyre in Winter A4
Head with Helmet A1, C38, E8
The Heights of Macchu Picchu B1, D3,
    E14
Her Lover, Mine A17
The Heraldic Vision C146
His Eyes Looking Forward and
    Upward C191
Home from the Nightless Summer
    A23
Homing Bones A2
The House of Leaves A17

I

I Have No Ireland C3
Ida Kar in Cuba C37
The Immigrant A19
An Immigrant's Address C184
In Memoriam: Kholiakov C199
In Such a Wind A2
In the Greenhouse C8
In the Scribner's Room A19, C135
The Indecision A19, C133
Insofar As No Hope Is Left to Him
    C206
Interludio Idilico: Coda D13
Interview C139
The Invisible Bride A14, C140
The Islands A2
Israel in the Park A1

J

JR/NT: Each to the Other A23, C159
The Joining of Hands A10
Jonah's Saddle A28, C200
Journal of the Laguna de San Ignacio
    A28, C162, C167
The Jubilation E36
July 4, 1976: Sevuokuk the Flight A23
The June Flower C191

K

Kadmon's Sister A19
Kenneth Patchen, Selected Poems B2
A Key to Human Communication
    C78
The King Returns C58
The Kitchen A14, C107, E25

L

Ladylike A17
The Lake A23

The Land in Question C205
Landscape Papers C150
The Landsongs A24
The Last Grand Rain C191
Last of the Chiefs A1, A3, C19, C41,
    C49, E11, E12
The Last Word: A Nobel for Neruda
    C102
A Latin Walt Whitman C100
The Laurel Tree A4, A5, C68, C76,
    C85
Leaving a Grandmother C48
La Légende de Sainte-Germain-des-Prés
    AP1
Letter from Homer A23, C168
Letter from Leningrad A16, A17
Leviathan D1
The Life Sitter C207
The Life We Do Not Lead A2, A3,
    C11, E9
The Light A19
Looking Back A2
Lying Beside Her C191
Lyrics for the Bride of God A14, C108,
    C116, C117, C122, C124, C125,
    C131, C137, C145, E21, E28, E32
*Lyrics for the Bride of God: Section: The
    Artemision* A12, C109, C111, C115,
    C123

M

Man D14
The Marching Columns C77
Marching Orders A23
Markings A4, E11
Master of the Name in His Privy,
    A.D. 1760 A1, C15
Master Spy A1, A3, C29, C38
Metamorphosis of Spider with Crab
    C199, C205, C208
Metaphors of Relative Elevation
    C175, E40
The Microcosm A19, C129, E16
The Ministry of Death A1, A3, A20
The Mountain A23

N

Narrative/Invocation of, and to, the
    Race Klukwan A23
Narrative of the Entrance to the
    Great North A23
Narrative of the Great Animal A23,
    C152, C166, E29
Narrative of the Heartbeat A23, C148
Narrative of the Readings in Chicago
    A17, C139
Narrative of the Spiders A17, C151,
    C160
Narrative of This Fall A16, A17
Narrative of This Fall A16, A17
Neruda and Indiginous Culture C204
Newfoundland C163
Newly Saying the Already Said C199
Nicodemus Speaking D5, D10
No se sentia bien D15
Noah on Ararat Again A1, A3
Nomad A1, A3
Non un passé mais un avenis C60
Nor Was It Possible C191
North Rim A28, C161, C179
The Northern Lover A19, C135
Not Asking the Way in a Park A1
Notes sur le thème de la diffusion C74
La Notte Oscura E18
The Novice A4
A Nowhere for Vallejo A10, A23,
    C90, C93, C97, C103, E12
A Nowhere for Vallejo, Choices, October
    A10
Numeros D15

O

An Obscure Meadow Lures Me D9
October A7, A23, C81, C82
October: The Silence A8
Of C163
Of a Marriage Made Within the
    Great Light C191
Old Savage/Young City A1
Old Savage/Young City A1, A3, A23,
    C31

The Oldest Guide C156
Olvido Inolvidable A16, C114, E19
The Omen A1, C21, C24
On Neruda C130
On Reading Song VI C4
On Seeing a Wheatear for the First
    Time C83
On the Way to Green Mountain A19
The Once and Future King C72
Open Letter Regarding a Proposal
    C162
Opening Out of a Line of Mandel-
    stam's C180, C188
The Opposing Coasts A17
Or That the President Would Abdi-
    cate A27, C186
Oregon Coast A23
Origin of the Order of St. Domingo
    A26
Out from Pennsylvania A23
Out of Sleep, Beyonded A1, C9

P

Pablo Neruda: Selected Poems B6, B7
Palenque A28, C170, C171
Pansies for Thought: Reflections on
    the Work of Claude Lévi Strauss
    C61
Paolo in Thule C88
Paolo's Dream A2, A3
Park, Tulpis, Wolves A2, A3
Pendant to the Earth A23, C147
Penguin Modern Poets 7 A3
Peredur West A27, C192
Perimeter A23
Persephone West C187
The Persephones A13, C107, C110, E36
Persephone's Down A1, C38
The Pictures A10
Piedra sellada D15
Poem Two (From: The Fire Poem) A15
Le Poète portugais Alberto de
    Lacerda C1
Poetry and Communication C50,
    C56
Poetry and the Cabala C25
Poetry Helplessly C27
The Poetry of Politics E11

The Poppies A19
Portrait of a Modern Jew A1, C28
Prayer for Roses Newly Planted A1,
    A23
A Preface E36
Projections for an Eagle Escaped A4,
    A23, C46, E12
Prototractatus C209
Provincial Morning A19, C126

R

A Rabbi's Dream A1
Rabinal-Achi: Part IV D12, E13
Rainer Werner Moves His Lady A27,
    C186
Ranger Spacecraft A1, A3, C136, E8
Reaching for Hölderlin C191
Recipts A17
Reconds of the Posthumous Life E25
Red Sea Passage C15
Redwoods A23
Reflector Interview C202
Regina v. Penguin C6
Remembering Benares A1, C7
Remission Bardo C205
René Grousset Weeping A1, C5, E27
René Magritte A17, C112
Requiem Pro Duabus Filis Israel A7,
    A10
The Residue A10
The Rights of Man A2, A3, C33, E9
The Ritual C189
Robert Redfield E38
The Rose from Ajusco A26
The Roses of Guatemala A17, C119

S

Salamanca, To A17
Sangha and State in Burma AP35
The Satellite A2, C53, C136, E8
Scorpions A10, C103
The Screens A10
Seeing American First C195
The Selection of Heaven C191

The Seven Years A17
She Becomes Our Lady C118
She Flies the Islands C99
She Is a Child C118
She Tears Him Apart C118
The Silence A10, E36
Simeon Bar Yohai A1, C15
Sin Alternativa A16, A17
So Long the Kenai A23
Sociologie C2
Some Peace from an Autumn Garden
  A1
Sparrow C163
Speaking with the Dead Along the
  Canal C191
The Square Root of Hip C79
The Stain A2, A3, C40
Standing Rock Sequence, The
  Dakotas A19, C135
Staying with the Laughlins A17
Stèles D2, D6, D20
Still Love with Republic A17
Summons of the Desirer D9
Svairye A18, A19
Swimmer A10, C103

To Certain, Mainly Younger,
  Women C126
To Meltzer at Bolinas A17, C98
To Tell Andrea of the Ile de France
  A1
To the Stillness of A1, C19, C54
Towards Any Geography A23, C118
The Traines A17
La Traviata A14
The Tree of Another World C180
Tres Desde Pachichiyut C120
Twenty Years Later D18
A Twilight for the Raj A1, C12
Twin Star to Persephone West C187
Two Poems from Wales C75

U

Under the Volcano C80
Union Mexicana de Organilleros A26

V

Valedictions C93, C94
Verse Letter to a Noble Person A17
Verses D8
Victor Segalen: Stelae B5
Virgo Speculatrix C32

T

Tactic A23, E31
Tajos C128
Taking Leave A10
The Tantric Tradition C62
Tepozteco, El A26
Terminal City A23
These New Cape Editions C63
Thinking Her Name A17, C121
Third Person E36
Thirteen to Bled A2
Thirty Thousand Years of Art C69
Those in Washington A17
The Thread as Before A17
Three Comings to the House of
  Leaves A17, C139
Three Months in Which to Live A25,
  C180
Three Poems A23
Three Proses C157
Thus Love C177
Time and the Highland Maya B10

W

The Walls of Santiago C119
The Wedding A1, A3, C20, C52, E9
Weekend in Mexico C174
Weekends in Mexico A26
Western Rivers A23
What We Have Known A23
Where Babylon Ends A2, A3, A4, C48,
  E34
The White Widow A27, C185
Willie Masters' Lonesome Wife C104
Willow C149, C169
Wind River Ballad A17

Winter Oasis C207
The Winter Princess A2, A4
The Work Laid Before Us E10

Y

You Are Becoming Near to Me C84
Your Age C67
Your House C65